Series editor: Philip Prowse

A Love for Life

Penny Hancock

CAMBRIDGE
UNIVERSITY PRESS

CAMBRIDGE UNIVERSITY PRESS

Cambridge, New York, Melbourne, Madrid, Cape Town, Singapore, São Paulo, Delhi

Cambridge University Press
The Edinburgh Building, Cambridge CB2 8RU, UK

www.cambridge.org
Information on this title: www.cambridge.org/9780521799461

© Cambridge University Press 2000

First published 2000
10th printing 2009

Printed in Italy by L.E.G.O. S.p.A.

A catalogue record for this publication is at

ISBN 978-0-521-79946-1 paperback
ISBN 978-0-521-68618-1 paperback pl

No character in this work is based on any person living or dead. Any resemblance to
an actual person or situation is purely accidental.

Contents

Characters

Fanella: an editor in a publishing company.
Steven: Fanella's ex-boyfriend.
Ellie: a five-year-old girl.
Teresa: Fanella's best friend.
Paulo: Teresa's husband.
Timothy: Teresa and Paulo's son.
Mark: a friend of Paulo's.
Rod: Ellie and Timothy's teacher.
Leah: Rod's wife.
Mrs Grey: the headmistress at Rod's school.
Mr Simpson: Rod and Leah's neighbour.
Norma: a woman who looks after Ellie.
Dan: a boy in Ellie and Timothy's class at school.
Mrs Bedrock: Dan's mother.

Chapter 1   *It's over*

'Teresa, I wondered if I could come round to see you. Something's happened.'

It was eight o'clock on a Monday evening. It wasn't the best time to telephone a friend with a young child. But this was a crisis and Fanella needed to speak to Teresa urgently.

'Of course you can come round,' said Teresa, 'if you don't mind giving Timothy a good night kiss. He'd be furious if he thought you'd been here and he hadn't seen you.'

Fanella smiled, swallowing back tears. She loved Teresa's little boy, but right now it was going to be difficult to see him. 'I'll be there in about ten minutes,' she said.

'Good,' said Teresa. 'See you soon then.' Fanella pushed her bike round to the front of her small house. She cycled across Cambridge, avoiding tourists and students as she went, unable to share the happy atmosphere everyone else seemed to be enjoying. The river was alive with boats, the grass full of people picnicking. It was June and the time for end-of-term dances and university ceremonies.

Fanella envied the younger people. They had so few worries. She was trying to fight back the tears that had threatened her all day at work, and were now clouding her eyes as she cycled.

She rang on Teresa's smart brass doorbell, parking her bike by the side of the large house.

'Come in,' said Teresa, opening the door. Her long

5

brown hair was piled on top of her head, and as usual she was dressed in jeans and a T-shirt. 'I think Timothy's still awake, and I promised you'd go up and say good night.'

Teresa always talked about her son before anything else. Fanella was used to it. She smiled and went straight up the stairs to the little boy's bedroom.

Timothy was lying in his bed flying imaginary aeroplanes through the air.

'I've come to say good night,' said Fanella, sitting down on his bed and thinking how much she liked him.

He looked so lovable, under the sheets in his clean pyjamas. The curtains were pulled to keep the summer evening light out.

'Is Mummy going out?' he asked. Fanella often looked after Timothy when his mother and father went out.

'Not tonight.' Fanella smiled. 'I've come to see your mummy. We're both here this evening.'

'Then I've got two mummies today,' he said, and Fanella laughed.

'I'm not your mummy,' said Fanella. 'I'm your special grown-up friend.'

'Whose mummy are you?' asked Timothy suddenly.

'Nobody's,' said Fanella, afraid the tears would start rolling down her cheeks again.

'Why not?' asked Timothy.

'Well, not all grown-ups are somebody's mummy,' began Fanella, feeling this whole subject was too much for her right now. 'Some grown-ups choose not to have children, and some grown-ups want to have children, but they can't.'

'Do you want to have children?' asked Timothy.

'Yes, I do, very much,' said Fanella, thinking how strange

it was that Timothy wanted to talk about this today of all days. 'Now it's time you went to sleep, and I'm going to go and talk to your mummy.'

Timothy put his arms up and Fanella leant over and kissed him on the cheek. Then he shut his eyes and began to breathe deeply. It was very pleasing, Fanella thought, when a little child trusted you enough to go to sleep in your presence.

She went down the stairs and into the kitchen where Teresa was putting dishes into the dishwasher. Fanella thought Teresa was so lucky. She had this large beautiful house, a happy marriage and a lovely little boy. But because Teresa was such a good friend, it was difficult to feel envious.

Fanella's own home was quite different. She loved where it was, in a busy area of the city. There was an Asian grocer's nearby, selling all kinds of food, and a pub at the end of the road.

But Fanella's house was tiny and she and Steven had done all the interior decoration themselves. In contrast to Teresa's soft shades of cream and natural wood, Fanella and Steven had gone a bit wild and had painted every room a bright colour, according to the mood they wanted to create. And always, in the back of Fanella's mind, had been the thought that one day, the little second bedroom would become her child's bedroom – the child she and Steven were going to adopt.

'Sit down,' said Teresa, waving a hand at the kitchen table. 'What would you like? Tea? Or something stronger?'

'Tea would be lovely,' said Fanella. 'I haven't had a thing since I got back from work.'

'Have something to eat,' said Teresa. 'There's some lasagne in the oven. Paulo's had to work late this evening. He just phoned to say he'd get something to eat on the way home.'

'No, thank you,' said Fanella. 'I couldn't eat anything. Just tea, thanks.'

'So,' said Teresa sitting down beside her friend, 'what's happened?'

Fanella took a deep breath. She wanted to tell Teresa the whole story without crying. But she could only manage two words. 'Steven's left,' she said.

'Left?' Teresa was horrified.

Fanella looked at her friend, and nodded. She swallowed hard.

'I can't believe it,' said Teresa. 'You two were so much in love. You could see it. Everyone could see it. What do you mean he's left?'

'Left,' repeated Fanella. 'He's moved out. He's gone to live in London. We've finished. Broken up. It's over.'

Teresa looked genuinely upset. 'What happened? When?'

'It's been going on for some time, actually,' said Fanella, feeling relieved now she had told Teresa. 'He's been seeing another woman. I don't think he really loves her or anything, but we've both been under so much stress with trying to adopt a child – I think he just cracked. This other woman was an escape route.'

'My goodness!' Teresa sat, not knowing what to say. This really had come as a shock to her. 'What . . . what about the adoption?' she asked, at last.

'It looks like that's out of the question now, doesn't it?'

said Fanella, holding her mug of tea tightly. 'The social services make it difficult enough to adopt a child when you're in a steady relationship. When they witness the relationship fall apart before their eyes, I expect they reject you immediately.'

Teresa couldn't help thinking this was probably true. She tried to think of some words of comfort for her friend, but found it difficult to know what to say. 'Fanella,' she sighed at last. 'I'm sorry. I'm truly sorry.'

'It's OK,' said Fanella. 'I just needed to be with someone this evening.'

'When did Steven leave?' asked Teresa.

'This morning. He came back last night from her house and told me he was moving in with her,' Fanella answered.

'Didn't he give you any warning at all?'

'Well, actually I knew about the other woman,' Fanella said. 'I've known for a few weeks. He started staying in London more and more. I guessed something was going on and I asked him. He said he was trying to stop the affair. I really believed him. He said it was one of those things that was difficult to end because he didn't want to hurt her. She's younger. She's only twenty-one, not ready to settle down or anything, and she doesn't want children yet. It's strange because, like me, Steven wanted children so badly. We were so close to getting one.'

Teresa looked at her friend and passed her a tissue. She knew all about the pain Fanella had gone through since she discovered she couldn't have her own children. Steven had been very understanding about it. He had moved in with Fanella and had lived with her for a few years before they decided to try to adopt a child.

Despite the difference in their lives, with Teresa now at home and Fanella still working at the publishers where they had met, the two women had remained close friends. Fanella and Steven had been very involved with Timothy ever since he was born. They had often looked after him, or taken him out at weekends. Fanella was never happier than when she was out with Steven and Timothy, imagining that one day it would be their own child who ran along between them. But now Fanella had to face the fact that the little second bedroom, reserved in her mind for the imaginary child, would probably remain empty forever.

Watching her friend, Teresa wanted to tell Fanella that there were other men out there. A lot of men found Fanella attractive. She was small, with a natural, country-girl face, short dark hair and dark brown eyes. She looked a little tired these days but that was hardly surprising, knowing what she'd been going through.

However, Teresa knew that Fanella did not want to hear this right now. Finding a man was one thing. Finding a man who was willing to accept that you could never have children, and who would support you through the difficult process of trying to adopt a child, was quite another. Steven had seemed perfect, but even he had weakened under the demands of the situation.

'The truth is,' Fanella went on, 'I can bear to live without Steven, I think, once I get used to the idea, but I cannot bear the thought of living without a child.'

'Timothy is almost your child,' Teresa said, putting her arm round her friend. 'He's always loved you. I sometimes feel he'd rather have you for a mother than me!'

Fanella knew Teresa was trying her best, but it didn't soften the terrible pain of not having her own child.

'I must go,' said Fanella, hearing Paulo's key in the lock. She didn't want to spoil the little bit of evening Teresa and her husband had left together. 'Thanks for listening. I don't know what I'd do without you.'

'I just wish I could help,' said Teresa sadly. 'Please come round any time you feel like it.'

As she watched Fanella cycle into the dusk, Teresa felt a little guilty at her own good fortune.

Chapter 2   *After the summer*

Rod woke up to the sound of the alarm clock. It was a Tuesday morning in September. The first day back at school after the long summer break.

He rolled over and looked at his beautiful wife. He admired her as she lay, still half asleep, on the white sheets beside him. It would be nice to stay in bed and spend the morning with her. But he had to be at school in time to prepare the day, before the children arrived at nine o'clock.

He rolled out of bed unwillingly and showered. Then, after pulling on the clothes he had put out the night before, he went down to the kitchen to make coffee. He would take Leah some coffee before he left, envying her being able to stay in bed in the mornings. She worked as a freelance interior designer and, unless she had an appointment somewhere, did not have to travel to work. She had a studio in the garage and operated her business from there.

Rod, on the other hand, had a forty-five-minute drive to the school in Cambridge where he worked. It was often a slow journey. The traffic seemed to get worse every day. But he and Leah loved their home in the country and, since he liked his job so much, the only option was to commute.

'I'll see you this evening,' he said, kissing his wife. She opened her eyes and smiled warmly.

'OK, have a good day,' she said, as she turned over and went quickly back to sleep.

An hour later, Rod was in his classroom and the children were arriving. You couldn't sit around for an hour in this job, catching up on phone calls, as you could in an office, Rod supposed. Children needed you then and there, and if you weren't prepared, the day could quickly turn into chaos.

'Morning, Rod.'

'Hi, Teresa. Hello, Timothy.'

Rod was Timothy's teacher, and Teresa was pleased. Rod was a good teacher and Timothy loved him. Rod was glad to have the little boy in his class and he liked Teresa; she was always friendly, and only ever had praise for the work he did.

Other parents were much more difficult. There was one mother who complained every morning about how her 'perfect little son', was being criticised by teachers and children alike. She could never see that her son might be to blame for anything. She even seemed to encourage him to start fights!

Rod could see this mother coming now, and tried to avoid her by capturing Teresa's attention. 'There's something you might be able to help me with,' he said to her. 'I want to invite someone in to talk about writing or illustrating children's books, or publishing them maybe. I thought it would be interesting for the children. I remember you used to work in publishing.'

'Ah,' said Teresa. 'I know just the person.'

'Good,' said Rod. 'Tell me more.'

'It's a friend of mine,' Teresa said. 'She's an editor for children's books and has a lot of contact with authors and illustrators. But, more importantly, she knows about the whole publishing process . . . and she loves children. I'm sure she'd be delighted to come in and give a talk.'

'Do you want to ask her first?' said Rod. 'If she's keen, she could telephone me at school.'

'OK. That sounds like a good idea,' said Teresa, kissing Timothy goodbye. 'She might be too busy of course, but I'll certainly ask her.'

'Thanks,' said Rod, smiling at her. 'Right,' he said turning to the class. 'Time to start the lesson.'

But the mother he had been trying to avoid was waiting for him. 'I want to talk to you about my Dan,' she said, ignoring the fact that Rod was trying to calm down thirty children. 'Dan told me that last term a boy called Timothy kicked him.'

'Last term?' Rod echoed. 'I really think that anything that happened over six weeks ago can be forgotten. We all want to make a new start at the beginning of the term, don't we?'

'There you go again. You teachers always have your favourites, while children like my Dan get blamed for everything,' the mother said.

'I'm not blaming Dan for anything,' said Rod sighing, and wishing the woman would go. 'I just want to start the new term off on a positive note. I'll keep a careful eye on the two boys today, and let you know if there's any trouble.'

Rod doubted that Timothy, who was such a quiet child, would have kicked Dan, who looked like a prizewinning boxer.

'You teachers. You just can't be bothered to do your jobs properly,' said the woman insultingly. 'I'll be asking my

14

Dan at the end of the day what happened, so you'd better keep your word.' She turned and left then, and Rod breathed a sigh of relief.

Rod enjoyed his job, and in contrast to the woman's accusations, he tried very hard to treat all the children fairly. But his job was made much more difficult when parents did not support him, and it always felt good when they did.

By lunchtime, he was already exhausted. One child had been sick, and had been sent home. Dan had got into trouble in the break for stealing another child's apple, then throwing it over the school fence. Rod had had to send Dan to the headteacher. Rod was sure Dan's mother would hear about the incident and would soon be back to complain.

'I need another holiday after this morning,' he joked to the other teachers in the staffroom. Several of them looked at him pityingly. Rod was the only male teacher and some of the women clearly didn't think he was able to teach six-year-olds as well as they could. One or two of them also thought that because he had no children of his own, he was even less qualified for the job.

'It's men, you see,' joked one of them now. 'You're just not up to it.'

Rod ignored her and went back to his classroom to prepare for the afternoon.

By three o'clock, as he read the class their afternoon story, they seemed much more settled. Looking at their small interested faces, he remembered what it was about the job he loved. However difficult they sometimes appeared, however awful their parents were, there was always some little ray of light in every child. Rod smiled to himself when he noticed that tough little Dan had his thumb in his mouth, as he listened to the story. Even Dan could be soft and sweet when he was tired and caught up in a good story, thought Rod.

Rod drove home, feeling the weight of the day lift from him as he left the city and set off across open country. His and Leah's home had been two cottages which they had made into one. With its views over open countryside and its stone floors and open fireplaces, it looked like something from a magazine. Leah had painted the walls white, stripped the paint off the wood and made her own curtains. Her antiques were carefully placed around the house, and everyone who came there admired it.

Rod liked the house too, but sometimes he couldn't help feeling it was maybe too elegant, too unlived in. He would be quite happy with a little more mess about the place. Leah placed high value on how things looked and for her the home was more important than anything. It was one of the reasons she didn't want children. She thought they would just mess it up and break her precious antiques.

But it certainly was a peaceful place after a long noisy day in the classroom. Rod pulled his shoes off and placed them carefully by the door. He walked across the stone floor in the kitchen to the drinks cupboard and poured himself a beer.

'Good day?' Leah appeared in the doorway, her blonde hair slightly untidy from bending over the drawings on her desk.

'Really busy,' said Rod. 'How was yours?'

'Great,' said Leah. 'I've been asked to redecorate the

Simpsons' farmhouse up the hill. It's a big job and they'll pay well.' She smiled. She loved her work and was beginning to get a name for herself in the world of interior design.

Rod admired her, and thought how different her days were to his. His day had involved dealing with a fight, a sick child, an anxious parent and a stressed headteacher, as well as trying to teach a group of children with hugely varying abilities. Meanwhile, his wife had done some drawings, visited a smart farmhouse and sat at her desk in the peace and quiet, looking beautiful. If he didn't love his job so much, he might envy her.

'I've made supper,' said Leah, opening the oven door and letting a delicious smell float into the air.

Still, thought Rod, as he sat back on the sofa, there was nothing nicer than coming home to a wife who enjoyed her job, and managed to cook a nice meal at the same time.

'It smells delicious,' he said, pulling Leah down onto the sofa next to him. 'Mmm, and so do you. What perfume are you wearing?'

'It's Chanel,' said Leah. 'A little treat for myself for getting that contract.'

'You deserve it,' said Rod, wondering when she'd had time to go into town and buy herself perfume. He was also feeling annoyed with himself – he wished he'd thought of buying it for her.

Chapter 3 *Instant attraction*

Teresa left Timothy's school that morning feeling on top of the world. She found Timothy's teacher very attractive. He wasn't like other teachers. Apart from the fact that he was a man (and most of the teachers in primary schools were women), he seemed to enjoy spending time with young children and took a genuine interest in them. She always liked people who were nice to her son, and in addition to this, Rod really was very good-looking!

She smiled to herself as she walked home. 'I have become a typical housewife,' she thought, 'fantasising about other men while my husband is out at work.'

But she didn't mind this image of herself. She enjoyed talking to Rod, and thinking about him made the day brighter until her own husband came home. She loved Paulo deeply, so a little romance was harmless. Anyway, Rod was married, and it was unlikely he ever gave Teresa a second thought. It was just nice to fantasise!

While she walked, she made a mental list of the things she had to do that day. She would shop at the supermarket for the week's food, and go into town to get some new clothes for Timothy. Then she remembered that she had to ring Fanella and see if she would go into Timothy's class to give a talk.

Teresa phoned Fanella at lunchtime, who agreed to call in on Teresa on her way home from work. Timothy was playing out in the garden with a friend when Fanella arrived at around six that evening.

'I was wondering,' said Teresa, pouring tea from a green pot into two patterned mugs, 'whether you'd like to come to Tim's school and give a talk on publishing children's books?'

Fanella took the mug of tea gratefully. She was thinking about Teresa's suggestion and wondering why Teresa had thought of asking her. Teresa was always thoughtful and kind to Fanella, but sometimes she had hidden motives for the plans she made. She wondered now whether this was just another way to make her feel part of Timothy's world. Fanella would love to share her knowledge with a class of children, but only as a professional publisher. She didn't want to do it just because Teresa felt sorry for her.

'Is this one of your ideas?' she asked suspiciously, looking at her friend through the steam from her tea.

'Not at all,' said Teresa. 'It was Rod's idea – you know, Timothy's teacher. He asked me this morning whether I knew of anyone, and I immediately thought of you. I told him you might be too busy. It would be doing him a favour of course.'

'Oh, I don't mind doing a school a favour,' said Fanella, 'as long as you're sure they want me. You're not just trying to cheer me up?'

'Oh, come on,' said Teresa. 'I know the last few months have been hard for you, but I think you're coping marvellously. So when do you think you might be able to go to the school?'

'I can take a day off next week. Ask him when he'd like me to come in.'

'I'll give you the school number, then you can talk to him yourself,' said Teresa.

'OK. Hey, is this the teacher you like, the one with the lovely eyes and black hair who looks like Tom Cruise?' Fanella asked.

Teresa laughed. 'Yes,' she said, 'it is. I think you'll find he's rather attractive. It's a shame he's married.'

'Oh, is he?' Fanella wasn't surprised. And anyway, she was not looking for a man in her life. They just caused you more problems, she had decided, and she was already managing very well on her own.

'By the way,' said Teresa suddenly, 'what's happening with that independent adoption agency you contacted?'

'Well,' began Fanella, cautiously, 'since the first interviews and workshops, I've had a team interview where they told me that being single shouldn't stop me from adopting. They want to make a home visit though, which is the most thorough part of the procedure, so nothing is definite yet.'

'That's great news!' said Teresa. 'And if I can do anything to help, I will – like telling them how wonderful you are with Timothy!'

'Thanks, Teresa. There's a long way to go yet of course: endless interviews, workshops and then there's the question of finding the right child. That's if they decide I can have one. But I'll need two references, so perhaps you could provide one of them.'

'I'd love to!' said Teresa.

Fanella cycled back to her own house feeling, for some reason, more optimistic than she had done for a while. Over the summer, she had gradually forced herself to stop thinking about Steven. She had redecorated her whole house so that it would no longer remind her of him. She had chosen the colours carefully, and just doing this had made her feel more in control of her life.

Steven had rung her once, to say he and his new girlfriend were planning to marry. Fanella had reacted by becoming even more determined to do the thing she most wanted to do: adopt a child. Steven was not going to stop her!

She had contacted an independent adoption agency the day after she heard Steven was getting married. She was told to go to an introductory meeting where she could learn more about the advantages and disadvantages of adopting a child as a single person. She had learnt that being single was not a problem any more – the important thing was your commitment to bringing up a child. Two interviews with a social worker had followed, and even though she still had to have a home visit and attend further workshops, she felt far more confident that she might be allowed to adopt a child.

Since then, she had put Steven out of her mind and concentrated on work and on finding out as much as she could about adoption. Now, in September, things did not look as bad as they had done that evening in June, when she had spent the evening in tears at Teresa's.

The next day Fanella phoned Rod at his school and arranged to go in the following week. Although she had to take a day off, she didn't mind giving the school her time. It would be a change for her to be with children, and interesting to see what happened inside primary schools these days.

A week later, Fanella arrived at the school. She was welcomed by the school secretary and given a cup of coffee in the staffroom. Then the secretary took her to Rod's classroom.

'Here you are,' said the secretary to Rod, as if Fanella was a parcel she was delivering.

Rod looked up from the child-sized chair where he sat, helping a group of children with some writing. Fanella's heart jumped. Teresa hadn't been exaggerating when she'd said Rod looked like Tom Cruise. But she hadn't mentioned his lovely warm smile and his gentle manner with the children.

Rod stood up, apologising to the children for having to interrupt their lesson, and came over to Fanella.

'Hi,' he said, smiling. 'Take a seat.' He indicated an armchair on the carpet. 'It's really kind of you to come in like this. Has anyone given you a coffee?'

'Oh yes, thank you,' said Fanella, sitting down and taking some pages out of her bag.

'Now, listen to me everybody,' said Rod, turning to his class. 'We're very lucky today because we have a visitor, a very special visitor, who helps to make the books we read in school. I'd like you all to come quietly and sit on the carpet, so she can tell you about her very important job.'

'I know her,' came Timothy's excited voice. 'I know you, don't I?' he said to Fanella.

Fanella smiled and touched his hair. 'You do, yes,' she said. Rod smiled at Fanella and her heart jumped again.

The talk went well. The children were very interested and sat with open mouths as Fanella showed them some original drawings, and compared them to the drawings in some published books.

'Everyone starts off making mistakes,' she told them. 'Sometimes artists try the same drawing ten or twenty times before they get it right. Put your hand up if sometimes you try a drawing and it comes out all wrong.'

A forest of hands shot into the air.

'Well, if you keep trying, like these artists do, you can get it right in the end,' she said.

She went on to talk about some of the authors she worked with. The children knew the names of some of them and were delighted to think Fanella had met them.

'That was great!' said Rod when Fanella had finished and the children had gone off for lunch. 'They were really interested, and it takes a lot to interest some of them!' He laughed. 'Hey, would you like to come for a quick lunch at the pub over the road? I'd like to talk to you more about publishing.'

'I'd love to,' said Fanella, thinking there was nothing she would like more right now.

They sat outside in the late summer sunshine, eating bread and cheese and drinking fruit juice.

'I'm going to tell you something,' said Rod, after they had chatted for a while about their different jobs.

Fanella looked at him, slightly surprised. What on earth was he going to tell her?

'I've written a couple of children's stories myself,' he said, 'and I wondered if you'd take a look at them?'

Fanella laughed with relief. 'I'd love to look at them,' she said. 'We're always looking for new talent.'

'Oh, thank you,' he said. 'I haven't actually shown them

to anyone else. I'm a bit embarrassed about them. They might be dreadful. But you must see a lot of dreadful attempts at writing for children, so you'll be used to it.'

Fanella laughed again. 'I do,' she said. 'But I'm sure yours won't be one of them.'

Rod smiled at her. For a brief second their eyes met. He noticed the deep brown of hers, the look of sadness, and felt suddenly that he'd like to know her better. But it was almost time for afternoon school to begin.

'Listen,' he said. 'I'll send you my stories at the publishers, shall I?'

'Be sure to address them to me personally, though,' said Fanella, 'or they'll be put in a pile somewhere and it'll be months before I get to see them.'

'OK,' said Rod. 'And hey, thank you again. You've made the children's day.'

'Goodness me!' thought Fanella as she cycled home. 'He really is quite something.' She was filled with a sense of joy she had not had for years, not even when she had first met Steven.

'He's the kind of man I could fall in love with,' she said to herself. But then she remembered: he was married and probably had children of his own. He was out of the question. 'I must focus on myself and the adoption,' she told herself.

But nothing could stop her heart from singing as she arrived home and went straight to the phone to ring Teresa.

Chapter 4 _An important visitor_

'You didn't tell me he was so attractive!'

'I thought I did,' said Teresa, a little concerned for Fanella. She hadn't heard her as excited as this for years.

'You said he looked like Tom Cruise, but you didn't tell me about that beautiful smile. Or about his sense of humour and the way he manages to talk to children without looking down on them and . . .'

'Hey, calm down, Fanella. I didn't tell you all that because I didn't want you to fall in love with him. He's married.'

'Are you sure?'

'Of course I'm sure! I've seen his wife,' Teresa said with a smile.

'What's she like?' Fanella asked.

'Tall, blonde, attractive, earns quite a lot of money as an interior designer. What other teacher do you know who drives a BMW?'

'Oh, I'm beginning to understand,' Fanella said, though she couldn't help feeling disappointed. There had definitely been something between her and Rod – she was sure of it. She couldn't help feeling he had liked her too. But it was clear from what Teresa had just said that he was very happily married. A rich blonde wife! He could hardly be attracted to a small lonely woman who wasn't even able to have children. She would have to forget about him.

'You must forget about him,' Teresa was saying at that

very moment. 'If I'd thought this would happen, I wouldn't have suggested you went in to give that talk. I thought you were more sensible than this!'

'I am, usually. I don't know what came over me!'

Teresa couldn't help feeling a little jealous at that moment. She had always thought Rod was a little attracted to her, as she was to him. But she stopped herself from feeling jealous. Rod was simply a really nice guy, and it wasn't surprising Fanella had got on well with him.

'Oh, Fanella!' she said. 'You've fallen in love with him! I should have predicted this. It's not good for you. You need to find someone single and available. You don't need any more problems in your life at the moment.'

'Oh, don't worry,' said Fanella. 'I'm not really looking for a man at all. I don't want anyone right now. I just couldn't help liking him. I shall forget about him the minute I put the phone down. I've got more important things to think about, like the social worker who is coming tomorrow evening.'

'Oh, yes, I'd forgotten. How are you feeling about that?'

'Nervous,' said Fanella, and she wasn't lying. It was going to be the hardest part yet of the adoption procedure.

She spent the rest of the day cleaning and polishing her house until it sparkled. At least there could be no question over the suitability of the home environment for a child. The hard physical work also helped her to forget about Rod. By the evening, she was concentrating once again on the possibility of becoming a parent, and had convinced herself to forget about romance for the moment.

Fanella had wanted children ever since her early

twenties. Now, approaching her mid-thirties, she felt a sense of urgency. She knew there were plenty of people who enjoyed successful careers, freedom and a good standard of living and didn't want a child. But, for Fanella, those things were not important. She wanted the deep commitment of a child, and she was prepared to sacrifice other things in her life for this.

The social worker was a thin woman, wearing grey clothes and with long grey hair tied up on top of her head. She stepped into Fanella's sitting room and immediately looked around, taking in the details of the small room.

'It's not a very big room,' she said. 'Have you imagined how much smaller it would feel, filled with children's toys? Children need space to move about too,' she added.

Fanella felt herself getting annoyed straight away. As if she hadn't thought about this! 'My friend's little boy loves playing here,' she said. 'He often comes with lots of toys and makes a whole world in here with roads and mountains and a garage.' She stopped, aware that she was sounding defensive.

The social worker didn't say anything, but quickly wrote something down. Fanella took a deep breath.

'Would you like tea, or coffee?' she asked, trying to relax.

'Coffee, white, two sugars,' said the social worker, sitting down on the sofa and continuing to write.

Fanella went into the kitchen. She was suddenly feeling very emotional. Ordinary parents didn't have to go through this exhausting procedure – it just didn't seem fair. All she knew was that she loved children and had the love to give a child who needed a parent. Everything else seemed irrelevant. Small room indeed! Children grew up in all kinds of conditions and survived. Surely, all that mattered was that they were loved?

She took the coffee through to the front room and sat down opposite the social worker.

'Have you considered what you would do about work if you were to adopt a child?' the woman asked her.

'I've given it a lot of thought,' said Fanella, truthfully. 'Obviously I need an income, as I'm single. I've been wondering, therefore, whether it might be possible to adopt an older, school-age child, rather than a baby. Then I could continue to work while the child was at school.'

'Mmm,' said the social worker doubtfully. 'Older children's personalities are far more developed of course, and adoptive parents often find they have very little influence over them. Remember, many of our children have had difficult lives and display disturbed behaviour patterns. Younger children haven't had as many problems in their lives, generally speaking, and you have a greater chance of healing some of their wounds.'

'It's not that I wouldn't want a younger child,' said Fanella, afraid suddenly that she didn't sound very motherly. 'It's just that, for practical reasons, an older child might benefit more from my situation. I don't want to adopt a child, and then get someone else to look after him or her. I want to do it myself.'

The social worker glanced at her and made some more notes. 'There are, of course, far more older children available for adoption, if you're prepared for the challenge,' the social worker said.

'Well,' said Fanella, feeling that the woman was softening, 'I know a school-age child would bring different problems, but I've thought about it. I find older children interesting.'

'You've obviously thought a lot about why you want to adopt a child,' the social worker continued, 'but have you ever thought of the problems adopting a child might bring?'

Fanella felt annoyed again. It really seemed as if this woman was trying to put her off. 'Well, yes,' she answered, trying to hide the note of impatience in her voice. 'This isn't just a casual idea. It's something I've been thinking about for several years.'

'Go on,' said the social worker.

'I'm aware of the sacrifices parents make, the heartache, the worry, the way a child changes their lives,' said Fanella with feeling. 'I've seen enough of it! I know you can't put your own needs first any more, once you have a child. No more last-minute evenings out or holidays abroad. I know that you have to be more responsible financially – you can't spend all your income on designer clothes! But I don't care about those things. I like being with children, the new view on life they give you. They can teach you a lot.'

'But what about, say, a child who shuts himself in his room and won't communicate with you?' asked the social worker. 'What would you do with a child like that? A happy child may well give you a new view on life. An unhappy one may simply wear you out with his misery.'

'Children are unhappy for a reason,' said Fanella, suddenly feeling exhausted. She hadn't prepared herself for this! When she and Steven had been interviewed together, the social worker had been much gentler with them.

'I'd try to understand the child,' she said. 'I hope I'd be

given some information about his past experiences so I could analyse what was going on and try to work with the child. And I'd only take on a child I felt I could love, through the good times and the bad.'

The social worker smiled. 'We'd only let you have a child we thought you could love,' she said. 'Now show me around the rest of your house, then we need to talk some more about your own childhood.'

By the time the social worker had left, Fanella was ready to fall into bed. It had all been much easier when Steven had been there to go through it with her. Then, they'd been able to share their answers, and talk about it and laugh together afterwards.

Now, Fanella felt lonelier than ever. The social worker had left without giving any clue as to what she was thinking. As far as Fanella knew, the social worker might have decided she was completely unsuitable to be a parent. Perhaps, she *was* unsuitable and had unrealistic expectations of herself.

She got into bed, trying to think of her life without a child in it. For so long it had seemed a possibility, on the horizon, as if everything else she did was leading to the point where a child would arrive in her life. Now, she thought that perhaps it was never to be.

No child, no Steven, no Rod. What else was there?

She buried her head under the sheets and closed her eyes. Suddenly she needed to sleep more than anything else in the world.

Chapter 5 *The decision*

Fanella wheeled her bike through the dark market square. It was decorated for Christmas and in the centre there was a large Christmas tree with lights.

Fanella's bicycle basket was full of presents. She would send some of them to her mother and father, who lived in the south of England, and some to her friends. She had decided to stay in Cambridge for the Christmas holiday. Although she would be alone in her house, she could mend the kitchen tap and the washing machine. She also wanted to buy some curtains for the second bedroom, just in case . . .

It was strange to think that this time last year she and Steven had planned Christmas together.

'It'll be such fun next year,' Steven had said, 'when we have our own child to share Christmas with!' And Fanella had agreed.

She couldn't help feeling sorry for herself now, as she thought how different the reality was. Here she was, a year older, not only still childless, but single as well. She had heard nothing definite from the adoption agency for weeks, although she had had several more visits from social workers and had attended some workshops. She was beginning to feel that everything was against her.

If they only understood how painful it was, not knowing whether you were ever going to be given a child to adopt. It had been so long since she had heard anything, that she had forced herself to stop thinking about it, at least until the New Year.

She opened the door, went into her sitting room and dropped the pile of presents on the floor. The house always felt so cold and unfriendly when she had been out all day. She rushed about closing curtains and turning on lamps. She put the heating on and plugged in the kettle. Then she noticed that the light on her answerphone was blinking at her.

Collapsing onto a cushion by the phone, she pressed the red button on the machine and sat back to listen to her messages.

'Hi Fanella. It's Teresa. I wondered if you'd like to come to Timothy's Christmas play with me at his school next week. Speak to you later!'

There was another message.

'Hello, this is the adoption agency. We've got some news for you. Please could you call us back as soon as possible.'

Fanella looked at the clock. It was six o'clock. She might be in time to talk to someone at the agency. But she was afraid of what they might say. She decided to call Teresa back first.

'I'd love to come to Timothy's play,' she told her friend. 'I can take the afternoon off work – everything's slowing down for Christmas now, anyway.'

'Oh good,' said Teresa. 'Timothy will be happy! He asked if you'd be there. He's a bit disappointed that he's not going to say anything. But if you're there to clap him, it will all be worthwhile.'

Fanella laughed.

Teresa continued: 'Yes, I think Rod felt he had to give the speaking parts to children who don't usually succeed at school. Rod's been having some trouble from one parent. She's accusing him of preferring the children who work hard and do well. It's all just gossip of course, poor man.'

'Well,' said Fanella, 'I suppose it's fair that less able children get a chance.'

'Oh yes,' said Teresa, sounding a little annoyed. 'Of course, but it shouldn't make the other children feel bad.'

'It must be very difficult to get the right balance,' said Fanella. She didn't want to argue with her friend, but she thought Rod was right to offer the speaking parts to children who didn't succeed in other subjects. She loved Timothy very much, but he was definitely a child who had lots of opportunities at home. All this helped him do well at school. He was always top of the class! It was good for him to learn, occasionally, to take a back seat and let children with fewer advantages do well.

'Anyway,' she added, 'we'll sit and cheer and clap when we see him, so he'll know that he's the best actor we've ever seen on stage!'

Teresa laughed. 'How are you anyway?' she asked.

'OK,' said Fanella slowly. 'Actually, I think the adoption agency may have some news for me. There was a message, but I don't know if it's good or bad. I can't bear to think about it. I've got to phone them back, but I'm too nervous!'

'Oh Fanella, I'm sure it'll be good news. It's so exciting! You must tell me as soon as you know!'

Fanella felt warmed by her friend's genuinely enthusiastic response, and a little guilty that she had been annoyed by her earlier in the conversation. 'Thanks, Teresa.

I hope I'll have some news by the time I see you at the play.'

'I'll look forward to it. See you then!'

'See you,' said Fanella and put the phone down.

Now there was no escaping the other phone call. Her heart was jumping as she dialled the number that had been left for her.

*   *   *

A few days later Fanella arrived at Timothy's school. The school hall was full of parents and young children. A large, brightly decorated Christmas tree stood in one corner. Fanella looked across the rows of heads for Teresa and saw her near the front of the hall.

'Just like Teresa to make sure she's got the best view!' Fanella thought.

As she squeezed past the other seats towards Teresa, she realised her friend was talking busily with someone. She reached Teresa's row and realised the person she was talking to was Rod! Fanella suddenly felt shy. It was months since their lunch in the pub together and she had put him completely out of her mind. But seeing him again, she couldn't help the same feeling of excitement she had experienced the first time she saw him.

Teresa looked up as Fanella arrived and put her arm round her friend. 'Here she is!' she said. So, Fanella had been the subject of their conversation!

'Hi!' said Rod, smiling warmly at Fanella. 'I must go. I've got to make sure everything is OK backstage! Good luck!' And he disappeared.

Fanella suddenly felt suspicious. 'Why did he say "good luck"?' she asked Teresa, sitting down in a seat beside her.

Teresa looked embarrassed. 'I hope you don't mind,' she said. 'I was telling him about your attempts at adoption. I've been so excited, I had to talk to someone about it! Now you must tell me . . . what's the news?'

Fanella was silent for a moment. She felt surprised that Teresa had been talking to Rod about her. At that moment, Teresa squeezed her arm.

'Hey!' she whispered, leaning towards Fanella. 'Look, that's Rod's wife!'

A tall blonde woman was walking down the side of the hall towards the stage. She stood out among all the other adults there. She was tall, slim and incredibly well-dressed. It was clear she didn't have children to look after and was used to more exciting things than a primary school Christmas play.

Fanella watched, interested, as the woman approached Rod. He leant towards her and kissed her on the cheek. Then they disappeared together behind the curtains by the stage. It was pointless worrying what Rod thought about her, Fanella realised, and pointless being angry with Teresa, who only wanted the best for her.

Fanella looked at Teresa. 'They've approved me for adoption,' she said, unable to hide a broad smile. 'And they say they've got a suitable child for me to visit after Christmas!'

'Fantastic!' said Teresa, clapping her hands together. 'I knew you could do it! Tell me more. Is it a baby? Boy or girl? What happens next?'

'Well,' said Fanella, not wanting to sound too excited, 'she's a five-year-old girl. People are looking after her at the moment and obviously it's better for her to stay there, where things are familiar, over Christmas. But the people she is with don't want to adopt her permanently. They find her . . . difficult, but the social services recommended me, because they thought I'd be able to look after her!'

'Difficult?' said Teresa, sounding a little concerned. 'In what way?'

'Well, she won't settle into school. She's been known to run away once or twice, and she's a bit difficult at home,' said Fanella. She didn't want to sound too negative about the child. 'But they feel she needs a lot of one-to-one attention. The family who are looking after her have three children of their own. She's found living with them difficult.'

Teresa sighed. 'I hope you aren't going to find it too hard,' she said.

'Well, nothing's definite yet,' said Fanella. 'I've got to meet and like the child first, and she's got to like me. I just feel pleased the agency believe I can do it.'

'Of course,' said Teresa, patting Fanella's arm affectionately, as the lights went off and the stage curtains opened showing ten little children. The child in the middle lifted his hand and waved. It was Timothy! Fanella and Teresa waved back as the music started.

Chapter 6 *Not an easy child*

The first time Fanella saw Ellie, she was standing on the top of a garden wall. It looked dangerous, and a woman was shouting angrily at her to come down.

Fanella looked at the small girl, balancing so high up, and was impressed by her grace and sense of balance. The situation was potentially dangerous, but the child looked so confident that Fanella herself was not alarmed.

Norma, the woman who was looking after Ellie, turned apologetically to Fanella. 'This is typical of Ellie's behaviour,' she said. 'It wears me out! But I suppose it's better if you see her as she really is, rather than dressed up and looking sweet and innocent. You need to know what to expect, if you decide to take her.'

Fanella nodded and smiled. She walked towards the wall and looked up into the little girl's face. It was a round pale face, with blue eyes, framed by blonde curly hair.

'Hi, Ellie. I'm Fanella,' she said gently. 'I've come to take you out, that is, if you'd like to come. I can see you're very good at climbing and balancing. Perhaps we could go to the park and you could show me what else you can do?'

Ellie stared at Fanella for a few minutes without altering her serious expression. Then, suddenly, she leant forward and jumped off the wall onto the grass. It was quite a long drop and Fanella couldn't help gasping in surprise. But she saw that Ellie had landed well and wasn't hurt.

'Get your coat, Ellie,' said Norma in a serious voice. 'Don't keep Fanella waiting.'

Fanella and the small girl exchanged a glance, and Fanella suddenly felt sure they were going to be friends.

It was strange spending an afternoon with a child she didn't know, but Fanella enjoyed it. It seemed to her that Ellie was not usually allowed to do what she was best at. Now that Fanella was giving her the freedom to run and climb and swing, she seemed like an uncaged bird. She played for hours, while Fanella sat on a bench and watched. Occasionally she got up to push her on a swing, or catch her as she slid down a pole. When it seemed that Ellie had had enough, Fanella suggested they went to a café and Ellie looked very excited.

Fanella had a cappuccino while Ellie had hot chocolate and a cake, and chatted to Fanella quite openly about her time with Norma's family.

'I like Norma, but her children can be annoying,' she told Fanella, biting into the cake. 'They often keep me awake at night with their games.'

'Don't you want to join in with their games?' asked Fanella.

'No!' said Ellie firmly. 'The boys fight all the time, and the girl plays with dolls. I hate dolls.'

'What do you like playing?' asked Fanella.

'I like playing with animals. I'm going to be a vet,' said Ellie. 'But sometimes I get so angry, I throw all the animals out of the window. Then Norma gets cross with me and says I'll never be a vet if I behave like that!'

Ellie was strangely adult in the way she spoke, as if she'd had too much experience of life for her age.

By the time Fanella returned her to Norma, she felt she'd got quite a good picture of the child, and had already grown very fond of her. Nothing was definite yet, but she could picture Ellie in her life already. She imagined taking her to all sorts of things she had never experienced before: the theatre, dance classes, gym classes, and possibly getting her a real pet to look after!

As she stood at the door ready to leave, Ellie came over to her and took her hand. 'Can I go with you now?' she asked, looking up into Fanella's face.

Fanella smiled and stroked her hair. 'Next time you're coming to see my house,' she said. 'It's only a week away. You must stay here until then.'

Ellie made a face, and Norma looked cross again.

'Come here and let Fanella go now,' she said. 'It's time for your bath.'

'No!' Ellie said and stood, not beside Norma, but beside Fanella. Norma stepped towards Ellie, but the little girl ran away from her and back towards the house. Once inside, she banged the door shut, leaving Fanella and Norma outside.

Norma pushed the door. 'She's locked it,' she said, glancing at Fanella to see how she was reacting to Ellie's behaviour. Fanella said nothing.

Norma pushed open the letterbox. 'Open the door now!' she shouted. 'Or you'll be going to bed with no supper!'

'No!' Ellie shouted back. 'I shan't open it. I can do what I like and you can't stop me!'

A few moments later there was a sound at an upstairs window and the two women looked up to see Ellie leaning out of the window with a glass of water.

'Get inside!' screamed Norma, alarmed that Ellie might hurt herself.

Ellie let go of the glass and it smashed on the path below.

'That's it!' said Norma, furiously. 'I'm going to get a ladder – I'll have to get in through the window.'

Once Norma had gone, Fanella called up to the window. 'Ellie,' she said softly, 'I understand exactly how you feel. You want to come with me, don't you? I understand because I really want you to come home with me now, too. We both have to wait, but it's only a week, Ellie and it'll pass very quickly, I promise.'

Ellie began to cry quietly.

'Come down, Ellie. Unlock the door and we can talk about it.'

Fanella watched the child, her heart racing: was she going to do as Fanella asked, or was she going to have another temper tantrum?

Slowly, the child withdrew from the window and, a few seconds later, Fanella heard the key in the door. By the time Norma returned with a ladder, Ellie was in Fanella's arms saying, 'sorry, sorry, sorry,' over and over again.

Fanella and Norma exchanged glances over the top of Ellie's head. It was clear Norma was not exaggerating when she said Ellie could be difficult in some ways, but Fanella wasn't put off.

'I'll see you next week,' she said, smiling down at the child, and turned towards her bicycle.

In many ways, it would have felt more natural to take the little girl with her there and then, because Fanella was sure that Ellie was the child for her. But there were legal details to sort out and strict rules to follow before she could keep Ellie. Ellie had to visit her house and see whether she liked it and would like to live there. If she did, she would move in on a trial basis for a few months before anything could be finalised.

It felt very lonely arriving home, and the house seemed even quieter than usual. For the first time in ages, Fanella thought about Steven and how much she missed him. She wanted to share this experience with someone – it felt so empty going through it alone. She ran herself a bath, poured lots of bubbles into it, got in and lay down, suddenly realising that this was what Ellie would be doing at that moment. She already felt close to the girl and wished she was here in the house with her.

*   *   *

A couple of months later, Fanella's wish had become reality. On the first morning after Ellie moved in with her, Fanella awoke, hardly able to believe there was a child in the second bedroom.

It was still early and only just getting light, but she got up and crept across the landing to look in at the bedroom door. Ellie's untidy hair covered the pillow. Her face, which displayed such adult expressions by day, was smooth and line-free in sleep. She looked almost like a baby, with her round cheeks, and Fanella had the urge to kiss her. But she didn't, not wanting to wake her from her peaceful sleep.

Instead, she went quietly downstairs and put some breakfast things on the kitchen table. She had bought cereal for the first time in years, in cardboard boxes advertising free plastic toy gifts inside. She had bought some fresh rolls and jam too, and lots of fruit. The sun came in through the kitchen window. It was March and the first shoots were appearing through the soil in the tiny back garden.

Fanella had booked theatre tickets for later that morning at the children's theatre nearby. There was a dance show on, which she was sure Ellie would enjoy. In the afternoon, she was going to take Ellie to meet Teresa and Timothy.

Suddenly her life felt full and interesting, and she realised how empty it had been for so long before this. As she sat and drank her coffee, she reminded herself that Ellie was still there on trial, nothing was official and it could all go wrong. The adoption agency could decide she was not the right mother for Ellie, or Ellie herself might decide she didn't want to stay.

Just then, there was a noise on the stairs and Ellie's face appeared round the door.

'Come and have some cereal,' Fanella said, pulling out a chair for Ellie.

Ellie sat in silence, pouring cereal into her bowl and then heaping it with sugar.

'Not too much sugar,' Fanella said. 'It's bad for your teeth, you know.'

Ellie looked at her and frowned. 'Norma let me have as much as I wanted,' she said, and Fanella realised there were going to be many occasions when she would be compared to Norma.

'I'm taking you to the theatre this morning,' Fanella said, deciding to ignore Ellie's remark. 'There are some dancers doing a show. I think you'll like it.'

Ellie said nothing as she ate her cereal. When she had finished, Fanella suggested she go and get dressed. Ellie sat in her chair, kicking the chair leg with her heel. For the first time since she had met the little girl, Fanella wasn't sure what to do and even felt a little afraid of the child whose moods seemed so unpredictable. Ellie hadn't looked at her or smiled since she had got up this morning, and Fanella felt afraid that perhaps Ellie didn't like her after all.

However, she quickly told herself that she was the adult, and that the child was having to cope with a new situation which must be very strange to her. It was no good being afraid of the child. She had to give Ellie a sense of security.

'I'll come upstairs with you,' Fanella said gently, 'and help you choose some clothes, OK? Come on.' She held out her hand towards Ellie. Slowly, Ellie took it in one of hers, and put the thumb of the other hand in her mouth. Saying nothing, she followed Fanella upstairs.

*   *   *

'She's not an easy child, is she?' Teresa said to Fanella that afternoon. They were sitting side by side on a park bench, watching Timothy and Ellie play. Ellie was faster and stronger than Timothy, and was clearly enjoying the fact she could climb higher on the climbing frame, go higher on the swing, and jump off higher things than Timothy.

Timothy watched the girl in quiet admiration. Ellie clearly enjoyed the fact he was impressed and began to show off more and more.

'Well, she's had a hard life,' Fanella reminded Teresa. 'I wouldn't expect her to be the most well-behaved child in the world.'

'Of course not,' said Teresa, but Fanella could hear a note of disapproval in Teresa's voice.

Fanella decided not to tell Teresa about Ellie's huge

tantrum that morning after the theatre, when she had wanted some sweets and Fanella had refused to buy them for her. She was longing to be able to talk to someone about it. But she was afraid Teresa would think Ellie was not the right child for her, if she pointed out any more problems.

As she walked home later that evening, with Ellie's hand in hers, she couldn't help but think what a very lonely job it was, taking on the responsibility for a child all by yourself.

When Ellie was finally in bed and she had kissed her good night, Fanella went downstairs to the sitting room feeling exhausted. To her surprise and concern she found she felt like crying! This was not how she was supposed to feel now she had a child in her life at last – she should be dancing with happiness.

But she couldn't stop the tears from flowing. She cried out of self-pity for her own loneliness, and out of pity for Ellie, who had had such a lot to deal with in her short life. She cried out of fear that perhaps, after all, she might not be able to cope with the child and all the mixed emotions she had brought with her. Normally, Fanella would pick up the phone and call Teresa, her best friend. But now even Teresa seemed difficult to talk to, since she clearly didn't understand why Fanella felt so attached to Ellie.

There is no-one else, Fanella said to herself, no-one, except me and Ellie.

Chapter 7 *Meeting Mark*

The Easter holidays were just beginning when Ellie came to live with Fanella.

'You'll have to go to school after the holidays, you know,' Fanella told Ellie.

Ellie looked at her and frowned. 'I hate school,' she said.

'Well, we're going to find you a new school, so perhaps you'll like that one,' Fanella said.

The local school was full and, anyway, Fanella had doubts about how well Ellie would fit in there. It was a large school with a lot of children in each class, and although Ellie was capable of standing up to them, Fanella felt sure she would be happier in a smaller class.

'Have you thought about Timothy's school?' Teresa asked her on the phone one morning. 'She could even go into Timothy's class. Rod is so good with problem children.'

Fanella was not sure how she should react to this comment. She did not consider Ellie a 'problem' child and felt upset that Teresa did.

On the other hand, she had a feeling that Rod, who she had seen teach and whose teaching style she admired, would get on very well with Ellie. Also, since there was no man in Ellie's life at home, it would be good for her to have a man teacher at school: it would provide some balance. The idea was not a bad one, and Fanella decided to phone the school later that day.

'By the way,' Teresa continued, 'I was wondering if you'd like to come to a dinner party next Saturday. You can bring Ellie. She and Timothy can watch a video in his room while we eat.'

Fanella smiled. It was typical of Teresa to think of everything. It was a long time since Fanella had been out in the evening. It would be good to spend time in adult company, knowing Ellie was safe nearby.

'I'd love to. Thanks, Teresa,' said Fanella.

'Timothy seems to like Ellie very much,' Teresa went on. 'He's always asking if she can come and play.'

'Ellie likes Timothy, too,' Fanella said. 'She'll really look forward to next Saturday.'

As she put the phone down, Fanella felt glad at the realisation that, no matter what Teresa said about Ellie, she was still a very good friend.

Fanella and Ellie cycled over to Teresa's house the next Saturday evening. Fanella had bought Ellie a second-hand bike and a bike helmet, and she was a good cyclist. Ellie was so pleased about the bicycle that she had been on her best behaviour ever since. Also, now she had got to know Timothy better, they had become good friends. When the door to Teresa's house opened, Timothy and Ellie ran straight upstairs together.

'This is Mark, a colleague of Paulo's,' Teresa said as Fanella entered the sitting room and Paulo put a glass of wine in her hand. 'And I think you know Mary and Simon. They've got a boy in Rod's class at the school.'

'Hello,' said Fanella, shyly. Mark was tall, blond and very good-looking. Fanella wondered whether he was married or had a partner. It was not often she met a good-looking single man these days. She felt self-conscious in front of him and turned instead to Mary and Simon, and asked them about the school.

'Oh, we highly recommend Rod as a teacher,' Mary said to Fanella, when she explained that Ellie would be going to the school. 'He's wonderful with the children. Billy loves him, and he's learnt such a lot since he's been in his class. He's rather attractive, too,' she said, smiling at her husband.

'Yes,' her husband replied. 'All the mothers are in love with their children's teacher, but he's married to a blonde beauty so we men feel quite safe.'

Mark was quiet. The conversation obviously didn't interest him and Fanella guessed he didn't have children. What she did not notice, however, when they sat down to eat, was that he was watching and admiring her. Mark liked strong women and he had decided that Fanella must be very brave to adopt a child on her own.

Later on, as they had coffee, Mark came and sat next to Fanella. 'It sounds as if you can't go out in the evenings now you've got a child,' he said, 'but perhaps we could have lunch together one day, when she's started school.'

Fanella was surprised. This was the first time a man had asked her on a date for years! 'Thank you, I'd enjoy that,' she said, feeling pleased and excited.

By the time she and Ellie left, she had arranged to meet Mark for lunch two weeks later at a restaurant overlooking the river. By then Ellie would have started school, and she would be back at work.

'So, what did you think?' asked Teresa on the phone on

Sunday morning, wanting to know whether Fanella was interested in Mark or not.

'He seems really nice,' said Fanella.

'I think he liked you, too.'

'Well, he asked me out to lunch, once Ellie's started school,' said Fanella.

'Oh good!' said Teresa. 'This could be the beginning of a beautiful relationship.'

Fanella wasn't so sure. It would be fun to go out with a man for a change, but a relationship would be a lot to take on at the moment, while she was still getting to know Ellie and her ways. It dawned on her that this had been a set-up: that Teresa had asked her on purpose, to introduce her to Mark. She didn't really mind as she knew that Teresa only wanted to help and only interfered in people's lives when she saw an opportunity to make them happier.

It was very strange approaching the school on Ellie's first morning. All the other mothers and fathers seemed to have been doing it for years. As it was her first day, Fanella wanted to take Ellie right into the classroom and make sure she settled in.

Rod was there, and she hoped to speak to him, to explain that Ellie was worried about getting lost and not knowing what to do. But he was deep in some kind of conversation – or was it an argument? – with another mother.

Fanella waited a while, finding that Rod's presence still caused her heart to race. She remembered what had been said at the dinner party, however, about how all the mothers were in love with Rod, and tried to pull herself together. At last he freed himself from the woman who had been shouting at him about something, and came over to Fanella, wiping his forehead.

'Hi, Ellie,' he said, speaking to the child first, which Fanella was grateful for.

Ellie smiled up shyly at him.

'Would you like to go and choose a reading book?' he asked her. 'Timothy will be here soon, and I think you already know him.'

Ellie did exactly as Rod asked her to do, and Fanella was able to explain some of her concerns to Rod out of the child's hearing. 'She's quite unpredictable sometimes,' she said to Rod, 'but it's because she's worried about doing the wrong thing. She doesn't mean to be badly-behaved.'

Rod smiled.

'It's just . . . ' Fanella went on nervously, finding it difficult to explain the child's character in a few sentences. 'If she isn't sure where she's meant to be, or what she's meant to be doing, she refuses to do anything. It can seem as if she's being moody. But if everything's made clear to her, she's very well-behaved.'

'Hey,' said Rod, squeezing Fanella's arm. 'Don't worry so much. I'm used to all sorts of children in here. I'm sure she'll be fine.' And he smiled at her in such a friendly way, her stomach did several turns. 'Come and see me at the end of the day,' he added, 'and I'll tell you how she got on.'

Fanella left feeling relieved and very lucky to have such a nice teacher for Ellie. She got to work feeling happier than she had done in ages. It was as if some of the anxiety over Ellie had been lifted a little, now she had shared it with someone.

She tried not to think it was also because she'd seen Rod

again and would see him every day now while Ellie was in his class. The thought of having lunch with Mark later on also made her cheerful, and she sang to herself throughout the morning. Several of her colleagues commented on her good mood.

'It certainly suits you being a mother,' one of them said. 'I haven't seen you look so well for ages!'

She was a little late arriving for her lunch date with Mark, and it was clear he was quite nervous. He must have thought that perhaps she wasn't going to come. He ordered drinks and they sat looking at each other across the table.

Fanella discovered it was very easy to talk to him. She told him all about Steven, and about Ellie, and about how hard it sometimes was being a single mother. Not just a single mother, but the mother of an adopted child. Mark listened and nodded, and Fanella found herself pouring out all her troubles to him.

He didn't tell her much about himself, apart from the fact he had worked with Paulo's company for several years, but had only recently moved to Cambridge and didn't know it very well.

By the end of the lunch, Fanella realised she would like to see him again. She wasn't sure if he would accept, but she took a deep breath and invited him over for dinner on Saturday night.

'I'll cook for you,' she said, feeling pleased to think it would be worth making an effort for a change. She had got into quite a boring routine lately, making simple meals for Ellie and eating the same food herself. It would be nice to cook something special, she thought.

Mark smiled at her. 'I'll look forward to that,' he said. Fanella, dizzy from drinking wine at lunchtime and excited at the thought of seeing Mark again, cycled back to work, smiling to herself all the way.

Chapter 8 *Trouble at school*

It had been a long hard week for Rod, but it was Friday morning and nearly the weekend.

Dan's mother really seemed to want to make trouble. She had been going on and on about a bruise on Dan's arm which she seemed to think was something to do with Rod, though Rod had never touched the boy. It was more than his job was worth to lay a finger on a child, however much they pushed your patience, as Dan certainly did. He was always starting fights, and it was hard not to physically pull him off the other children.

Rod parked his BMW in the school car park and went to get his classroom ready. He was looking forward to this evening. Leah and he were going to the theatre and out for a meal. Then they were going to have a quiet weekend together. They had both been so busy lately, they had hardly seen each other.

Rod smiled as he saw Fanella approaching the classroom with Ellie. Ellie was a lovely child, a real character. He wondered why Fanella worried so much about her, though he supposed she was still getting used to being a parent. It must be hard, he reflected, doing it on your own, especially if the child is not yours biologically.

Ellie really seemed to enjoy coming to school. She always went straight to the book corner, chose a reading book and settled down without being asked. Fanella was therefore much more relaxed about leaving her than she had been that first morning.

She smiled and waved as she left, and the other children began to arrive. When Rod called out the children's names and wrote in the register, he was quite pleased to see that Dan was absent. It meant there would be fewer conflicts and he would have a nicer day.

Rod was just looking forward to his cup of coffee when there was a knock on the classroom door and the headteacher, Mrs Grey, walked quickly in. She was a tall woman with a sharp brown haircut.

'I need to see you in my room at break time,' she said and disappeared again.

Rod cursed silently. Once the head got you in her office, she liked a good long chat and you could say goodbye to your morning coffee. When it was time, he sent the children outside for break and went and knocked on the headteacher's door. She looked at him seriously across her desk.

'I'm really sorry about this and I don't want you to think for a minute that I believe what has been said,' she began. 'But there are legal procedures and we have to follow them.'

Rod frowned and his heart jumped a little. This sounded serious and he had a horrible feeling it might have something to do with Dan and his mother.

The head took a deep breath. 'I've had a phone call from Mrs Bedrock, Dan's mother,' she said. 'I expect you've noticed Dan's not at school today.'

'Yes, it's quite a relief, actually,' said Rod, hoping the

head would share his humour. But she looked at him even more seriously.

'Apparently, Dan has accused you of bruising his arm and trying to hurt him,' said Mrs Grey, looking at Rod.

Rod raised his hands in despair. 'This has been going on all week!' he said. 'His mother has been on and on about that bruise on his arm which, as far as I know, he got fighting with Tom one break time. She wants to make trouble this term. She thinks I favour the other children, but she won't listen when I tell her Dan's behaviour is getting worse and that he needs some extra support.'

'I know, I know,' sighed Mrs Grey. 'I know Dan and his mother as well as you do. You're not the first teacher she's given this kind of trouble to. But I'm afraid she's gone to the local education authority this time. This means we have no choice but to suspend you until you are proved innocent in a disciplinary hearing.'

'Suspend me?' Rod said in disbelief.

'Yes, I'm afraid so,' continued Mrs Grey. 'You'll have to stop teaching for a while. You'll still be paid of course, but you must leave the school until this incident is sorted out.'

Rod was silent. He couldn't believe what he was hearing. Suspend him! He hadn't done anything! Never had he felt so unfairly treated. He had spent a large part of the school year trying to find positive things to say about Dan, and had even given him the star role in the Christmas play.

Slowly, he began to realise that if he was suspended from the school, his reputation would be damaged forever, even if he was eventually proved innocent.

'I want you to know that I do not believe the accusation,' said Mrs Grey. 'I have every confidence in you as a member of my staff, and I consider it a huge loss that we should have to do without you for any time at all. However, I really don't have a choice.'

Rod got up. 'I'd better get back to class,' he said.

'No, Rod. I'm afraid we have to suspend you right now. You'll have to go home. I'll be taking your class for the rest of the day, and we'll get a temporary teacher for next week, or the next few weeks, if necessary.'

Rod looked at her. He could see how sorry she was – it was written right across her face – but it was clear there wasn't going to be an easy way out of this.

He went back to his classroom to pick up his bags and coat, then walked quickly, head bent, to the car park. Ellie and Timothy ran after him.

'Where are you going, sir?' they asked, as he fitted his key in the lock.

He looked at their eager, friendly faces as he climbed into the driver's seat. 'I've got to go home,' he said. 'Mrs Grey will teach you for the rest of the day.'

And he swallowed hard as he watched their disappointed faces in his rear view mirror as he pulled out of the school gates.

He drove fast out of town. At least at this time of day traffic was light, and it was a relief to be in open countryside. It felt strange to be outside school in the middle of the morning. He could hardly believe what had happened. He knew that part of it was to do with his being a man. Women teachers rarely got accused of child abuse; men were always going to court for it.

What he couldn't work out was why Dan's mother was so determined to believe her son. Surely she knew Dan was making it up to hide the fact he had been in another fight? Did she realise the consequences for Rod, as a teacher, and if she did, why was she so determined to get rid of him? He had really done his best to be patient with both her and her son – she must realise this!

Then he thought about the other children in the class, the children he had given so much time and attention to this year. He thought of Ellie, how attached to him she seemed to be and how she did not deserve any more instability in her life. It was a terrible situation for everybody.

As he pulled up outside his house, he wondered how Leah would react to his being home at this time of day. He knew she enjoyed having the house to herself; they had once talked about how hard it would be if they both worked at home.

He pushed open the door and called her name, but there was no reply. She must be working in the garage or perhaps she was out with a client. He put the kettle on – he hadn't even had his coffee that morning – and put some coffee into the coffee pot. Then he went out to the garage to see if Leah was there.

She was there, bent over some plans on her desk. 'What on earth are you doing home?' she asked, not looking exactly pleased to see him.

His heart sank. He needed her, at least, to be kind to him today. 'Something's happened,' he said in a low voice. 'I don't suppose you could take a coffee break and come and talk to me in the kitchen?'

Leah looked rather annoyed. 'I've got this to finish by lunchtime,' she said. 'Is it some kind of crisis?'

'Yes,' said Rod.

Leah glanced back at her papers, then got up. 'I guess I can take a few minutes,' she said, seeing the desperate look on her husband's face.

They went into the kitchen together and Rod finished making the coffee. Then he related the story to Leah.

'So I had to leave right then,' he finished, 'and come home. I don't know how long it's going to take to sort this thing out, but until they get to the bottom of it, I'm afraid I'll be at home.'

Leah patted him sympathetically on the shoulder and then looked at him questioningly, 'And . . . you didn't?' she asked.

'Didn't what?' asked Rod.

'Hurt the boy?'

Rod looked at Leah in shock. 'Leah!' he said. 'How could you even ask that?'

'It's just that, in your situation, I know I would sometimes feel like giving one of those children a good hard slap!' she said. 'They must drive you mad!'

Rod looked at the woman he lived with and wondered suddenly whether they really knew each other at all. 'No,' he said coldly. 'I didn't touch the boy.'

'Well,' said Leah, getting up, 'then surely this will soon be sorted out and you can go back to work. Don't worry, darling,' she added, kissing him on the cheek. 'At least you can have a rest – you certainly need it. Now, I must get back to work. I've got an appointment at lunchtime.' And she disappeared back to the garage.

Chapter 9 *A difficult period*

On Saturday evening, as she cooked in the kitchen, Fanella was feeling very nervous about seeing Mark. Ellie was in the front room watching a video, something Fanella felt a bit guilty about. She had never agreed with people who thought it was all right for children to watch endless TV. But she was beginning to realise that there were times when a good children's video worked wonders for a tired child, as well as a tired parent! They'd had a busy day, having been swimming and shopping round town, and Ellie had been in an emotional state when they got home.

She had cried when she heard Fanella was having a grown-up friend for dinner, saying she didn't want him to come. Fanella guessed this had something to do with the changes at school that week – Rod hadn't been there and a temporary teacher had replaced him. Ellie liked things to be predictable and she also liked Rod: no other teacher was as good as him in her view.

So when Fanella told Ellie she was going to meet someone new this evening, it was more than the child could take. Fanella had solved the situation by suggesting they hire a video and Ellie had chosen Disney's *Cinderella*, which she was now watching. However, Fanella rather wished Mark wasn't coming, so that she could spend all evening with Ellie and then go to bed herself, as she was feeling quite exhausted.

Ellie was in bed by the time Mark arrived, but it was not long before her curly head appeared round the sitting-room door. She obviously wanted to have a look at Fanella's new friend.

Mark didn't seem too pleased to see the child and made very little effort to talk to her. Fanella began to feel uncomfortable. 'Go back to bed Ellie,' she said. 'I'll come up for a moment.'

She thought how different it would have been if Mark had offered to read to Ellie, so she could get on with preparing the meal. But he simply stretched his legs out and sat back in his chair with his drink while Fanella took Ellie back upstairs. Ellie was not going to give in easily. 'I'm not tired,' she said. 'Can I come downstairs and watch another video?'

'No,' said Fanella firmly. 'You *are* tired. Perhaps you don't think you are, but you've had a busy day.'

'Will you read me a story?' asked Ellie.

'Well, I need to go and get dinner ready. I'll just read you a short one.'

But by the time she had read Ellie a story and fetched her a drink, a smell of burning was drifting up the stairs. 'Oh no!' cried Fanella. 'That's the food! It'll be ruined!'

She rushed down, just in time to save the meal she had carefully prepared from going up in flames. Mark ate politely, saying it was very nice, but Fanella felt embarrassed.

'Shouldn't you try and get her to bed earlier?' Mark asked her. 'Children always push their luck if you give them a chance.'

It turned out he had two children of his own, who lived

with their mother and who he only saw every month. He'd separated from his wife three years ago and she lived in Devon, so he couldn't see his children more often. 'But I don't mind,' he said. 'We have a good time when I do see them, and the rest of the time I'm a free man!'

Fanella couldn't help wondering what the children felt about this arrangement, but she said nothing. She wasn't sure what to make of Mark. He was quiet and a good listener, but there was something a bit unkind about his attitude, both to Ellie and to his own children, that gave her reservations about him.

After the meal, she found herself wishing he would just leave so that she could go to bed, and she had to drop several hints about how tired she was. 'I'm not exactly making myself attractive to him,' she thought, 'going on about how tired I am, but I really do want to go to sleep.' She was afraid the evening had been a disaster, and that he would never want to see her again.

But he stopped in the doorway as he was about to leave, and bent down to kiss her. His kiss was gentle, and suddenly Fanella wondered whether it was a mistake sending him away like this. 'Can I see you again?' he asked, to her surprise, and she was quite glad to be asked.

'Perhaps another lunch would be easier,' she said, smiling, and he nodded.

When he had gone, she went straight up to bed but found she couldn't sleep. Too many thoughts were flying through her head. Did Mark want to have a relationship with her? Did she want to have a relationship with Mark? And, if so, how would Ellie feel about it? Was Ellie going to be more difficult, now she knew Fanella better?

Why was Rod away from school? Would he ever come back?

As she began to drift into sleep, she dreamt that she was standing laughing in a park watching Ellie playing happily and that Mark had his arm around her. She felt complete for the first time in years, as if all her worries had floated away. She turned to look into the man's face, only to find that the man was not Mark at all, but Rod.

*　　*　　*

Fanella had guessed correctly that this might be the beginning of a difficult period for Ellie. It was clear Rod wasn't coming back to school very quickly. The parents were told the temporary teacher was going to continue until half term at least, but they weren't told why. Ellie had taken a real dislike to this teacher and was refusing to go to school in the mornings.

'I just don't know what to do,' Fanella said in desperation on the phone to Teresa. 'Can I come and talk to you?'

It was a long time since she and Teresa had had a chance to talk on their own together.

'Yes, come round. Come for lunch,' said Teresa eagerly. She found her days alone at home long and lonely sometimes, and was glad at the thought of some company.

Fanella took some wine and went round to Teresa's house.

'All children behave like that at times,' Teresa told her. 'You mustn't think it's to do with her being adopted.'

'It's just, well, she seemed to settle in so quickly with Rod, and now she seems to be going backwards. What does Timothy think of the temporary teacher?'

'He says she shouts sometimes, and is stricter than Rod, but it doesn't worry him,' said Teresa.

'What's the matter with Rod?' Fanella asked. 'Have you heard anything? Is he ill?'

'Well,' said Teresa slowly, obviously enjoying the fact she had news to tell. 'The gossip going around is that he hit that boy Dan hard enough to bruise him. Dan's mother went to the education authority and accused Rod of abusing her son. They had no choice but to suspend him immediately, until a court hearing finds him innocent, if they do . . . '

'But that's terrible!' said Fanella, with feeling. 'Rod could never have done a thing like that!'

'Well, that's what most of us think,' said Teresa. 'But of course, there are those who say they wouldn't blame him for hitting that child. Dan's the kind of boy who would drive the most patient person in the world wild.'

'But Rod is so professional and so gentle. I could imagine some people losing their heads and doing something silly, but not Rod.'

'Hmm,' said Teresa, sighing, and placing a plate of salad in front of Fanella. 'It can't be doing his career much good, even if he *is* innocent, having this kind of scandal going round Cambridge.'

'We really ought to do something to help him,' said Fanella. 'He is being treated so unfairly.'

'It's difficult to prove that he is innocent though,' said Teresa. 'The education authority places a lot of importance on what the child says.'

'Why would the child want to lie like that?' asked Fanella.

'That's the big question,' said Teresa. 'Of course, he may not be lying.'

'I'm certain he must be,' said Fanella, 'and it makes me so angry. Not with the child, he's probably just doing what his mother tells him to do. Is there some reason why she might not like Rod?'

'Well, she's one of the mothers who thinks he favours the rich kids,' said Teresa. 'She thinks he doesn't like her son because he's from a poor background.'

'That's not true. Rod likes Ellie and she's not rich.'

'We know it's not true,' said Teresa. 'But some people get fixed ideas about things like this. Anyway, I hope you aren't so upset about this because you're still in love with Rod?'

'No!' said Fanella, a little too angrily. 'I'm upset for Rod, and because his absence is giving me problems with Ellie just when I thought she'd settled down.'

Teresa looked at Fanella suspiciously. She knew her friend too well to be completely fooled by what she was saying and felt slightly annoyed by the fact Fanella was obviously still attracted to Rod. She didn't know why it annoyed her. After all, she'd always had a similar feeling about him. It was just that Fanella always seemed so serious about things, while Teresa had felt quite light-hearted about her attraction to Rod.

'How's it going with Mark, anyway?' she asked, deciding the best thing was to get Fanella off the subject of Rod.

Fanella hesitated. 'I'm not sure,' she said. 'He's nice, and attractive, but I don't think he's got much time for Ellie.'

'It's you he should have time for,' said Teresa. 'You can't put Ellie first in every area of your life. If you get on well with him, she'll find a way of fitting in.'

'I'm seeing him again next week,' said Fanella, not really wanting to talk about it. 'So I guess I'll see how we get on then.'

Teresa smiled. 'He's very good-looking isn't he?' she said. 'Handsome and rich. You could do worse. Anyway, I think you should stop worrying about Ellie. She'll be fine once she gets used to this new teacher. Why don't we take her and Timothy out this weekend and you could bring Mark?'

'Maybe,' said Fanella. 'I'll give him a ring and see if he's free.'

But as she left Teresa's house, she realised she felt no better than when she'd arrived. The things she'd heard about Rod had really upset her. They couldn't be true! If they were, it meant she'd completely misjudged his character, and she was usually pretty good at judging character. It also seemed unlikely he would be back at school very soon. Whatever Teresa said, she doubted if Ellie was going to get used to the temporary teacher.

She decided the only thing to do was to concentrate on her work, or she would go mad with worrying.

Chapter 10 *The brown envelope*

Things were going badly for Rod. It was another month until the court hearing and, in the meantime, he had been interviewed by various people trying to establish the facts. His lawyer believed they could win the case, but there was no doubt the whole business would damage his reputation.

He didn't enjoy being at home every day either, and Leah obviously wanted the house back to herself.

'Can't you apply for another job?' she asked him one morning, finding him in his dressing gown in the kitchen at ten o'clock in the morning. She was dressed up to go out to an appointment and smelt of that lovely perfume again, but this time Rod had no desire to comment.

'I don't want another job,' he said. 'I want my old job.'

'I don't understand it,' said Leah. 'It was stressful, you've been treated so badly and, anyway, working with kids is my idea of hell!'

'Well, we're different in that way!' said Rod. 'I loved some of those children. I really felt I could make a difference to their lives.'

'Don't get emotional,' said Leah.

'Perhaps if we had a child of our own, you'd understand a bit better,' said Rod.

This had become the cause of many arguments between them lately. Being at home every day had made Rod think about what it would be like to have their own child. A lot of men stayed at home to bring up children these days, and it was something he thought he would enjoy. But Leah didn't want children. This hadn't worried Rod before, but now, as he approached forty, he realised how much he wanted his own child. He couldn't understand how Leah could be so sure she didn't want them.

Once she had left for her meeting, Rod went upstairs to get dressed. Then he noticed a heap of papers in the corner of the bedroom. He bent down to pick them up and realised they were the children's stories he had tried to write. He'd been so busy over the last few months, he had completely forgotten about them!

He sat on the bed reading through them, and thought they were not too bad. Then he remembered that he had asked Fanella if she would look at them. Suddenly he felt better. He would spend the day going through the stories, making corrections and improving them. It would give him a focus to his day.

He got dressed quickly and went downstairs to sit at the kitchen table. He worked eagerly all day, until he heard Leah's key in the lock at seven o'clock.

'Ooh, what's this?' she said, leaning over his shoulder and looking at the story which lay on the top of the pile. 'Children's stories! Haven't you had enough of children? Have you made any supper?'

'I've been too busy, I'm afraid,' said Rod.

'Busy! You've nothing to do all day!' she said crossly. 'I've come in tired and stressed, hoping my supper would be ready!'

Rod sighed. He realised he could have made supper, but he had been too involved in his stories to give it any thought. Leah always seemed annoyed with him these days, whatever he did.

'I'll go out and get a takeaway,' he said, trying to please her. He put his arms around her and kissed her. She smelt as lovely as ever, but she moved away from him quickly.

'Yes, OK. I fancy something Indian,' she said. 'Can you get a curry?'

'Anything for you!' said Rod, and to his relief she smiled, briefly.

Over the next few days, Rod worked enthusiastically on his stories. He had not realised how much time it would take to get them into shape. At last he felt they were good enough to be read by someone else. He wished he'd had the chance to try them out on his class before he posted them. Instead, he had to imagine the children in his class and their reactions to the stories. This helped quite a bit, and he couldn't help believing there was some potential in them.

If nothing else, it had taken his mind off the subject of Dan and his mother and given a purpose to his day. When he finally posted the stories, he felt a huge sense of achievement: even if no-one else liked them, he'd done it!

Meanwhile, Fanella was struggling with the problem of what to do with Ellie. She had found the best method of dealing with her not wanting to go to school was to drop her off in the morning and leave straight away. If she hung around for long, Ellie would hold onto her, making the whole thing worse. The possibility that the legalisation of the adoption would not be finalised, if it was seen that Ellie wasn't happy, was always at the back of her mind. Yet, despite the heartache Ellie gave her, Fanella had grown to love her dearly, and she couldn't bear the thought of not having her in her life permanently.

Quite often, in the mornings, Ellie would crawl into bed beside Fanella and together they would read or listen to the radio until it was time to get up. And at the weekends they had a great time together. It was only school that threw a shadow over their life together.

To stop herself from worrying, Fanella concentrated on her work. She felt a sense of relief as she left the school for the more peaceful atmosphere of the office. Then she worked hard until it was time to go and pick Ellie up from the club she attended after school.

One morning, as she arrived at the office, she was surprised to find a large brown envelope sitting on her desk. 'For the Personal Attention of Fanella Browning' was written in capital letters across the top.

It took her a little while to realise who the bundle of stories was from. She had completely forgotten about her conversation with Rod in the pub garden last September, when he'd told her that he'd written some stories for children. It felt strange to have them here in front of her, when she hadn't seen him for so long and knowing what he'd been accused of. But she was pleased he'd sent them.

Looking through them, she was impressed. Rod clearly had an understanding of what interested children; his language was appropriate and the stories had an originality which would make them sell. She was quite excited to have them, although she knew there were a number of stages to go through before she could offer him a contract. She would have to take them to an editorial meeting, then to a sales meeting, and get approval from both of these. But in the meantime, there were a few changes she would like him to make. She would have to arrange a meeting with him, too!

His phone number was at the top of the letter and later that day she dialled it. Her heart beat loudly as she waited for his reply, and she realised she was shaking as he picked up the phone. This was ridiculous! She was simply performing a professional task.

'It's Fanella,' she said, not sure whether she should use her surname too, to give a more professional feel to the phone call. But it seemed silly to be too formal when she had seen him every morning a few weeks ago at school.

'Hi!' he said, sounding a little shy himself.

'I received your stories,' went on Fanella, feeling more confident now. 'I liked them very much,' she said. 'But there are a few changes we'll need to discuss before I can offer you a contract.'

'Oh, that's great!' said Rod. He hadn't expected such a quick reply to his letter, and he certainly hadn't been at all confident about his stories being well received. Of course, it helped that he'd met Fanella, and he hoped she wasn't just being kind to him because he'd taught her child. He realised she'd probably heard about the accusation that he'd hit Dan and he wondered what she thought about it.

'Can you come to the office for lunch . . . or . . . come to think of it, we could meet somewhere more convenient, a restaurant or something?' said Fanella. It felt strange, as if she was asking him out on a date.

'I'm new to this,' said Rod. 'You decide.'

'Shall we meet next Tuesday at Brown's?' asked Fanella.

She liked Brown's. It was always busy, but the food was good and the tables big enough to work at.

'OK,' said Rod. 'That sounds fine. What time?'

'Let's say . . . ' Fanella did a quick mental calculation in her head. If she made it too late, they would not have much time together before she had to pick Ellie up from school. 'Shall we say twelve-thirty?'

'Great!' said Rod. 'I'll see you then!'

'Wow!' thought Fanella. 'Lunch with Rod!'

The fact that it was a professional meeting did nothing to stop her excitement at the thought of seeing him again for the first time in weeks.

Chapter 11 *Lunch with Rod*

It was a wet morning. The rain poured down. Fanella had cycled to work and had planned to cycle to the restaurant to meet Rod, but now realised she would arrive looking a mess. She decided to get there early, so that she could tidy herself up in the cloakroom before Rod arrived.

By the time he did turn up, ten minutes late, she was feeling calm. She had already had a Martini to calm her nerves and she ordered Rod an orange juice at his request. They then sat and looked at each other across the table for a few seconds before Fanella spoke.

'I must say that I'm very sorry you've not been at school these last few weeks,' she began, wanting to get the subject out of the way quickly. 'Ellie has missed you a lot. You really helped her settle in, and she's been taken back a few steps by the temporary teacher who doesn't seem to have your patience.'

Rod smiled sadly. 'It's been a difficult time for me, too,' he said. 'It's the last thing I wanted for Ellie or for any of the children. But schools are required to follow procedures in cases like this: it's to protect the children.'

'Yes, I know,' said Fanella. 'But it isn't protecting them if you didn't do anything wrong. It's doing them more harm than good.'

'Well, hopefully, once there's been a court hearing, I'll be back,' said Rod.

Fanella smiled. 'I'm sure you will,' she said. 'Most of the parents are behind you.'

Rod smiled again, appreciatively. 'I hope you're right,' he said. It was the first contact he'd had with any of the parents since his suspension, and he suddenly realised what an enormous relief it was to be able to mention the subject. In his mind, everyone had turned against him. The reality was clearly quite different.

Fanella, aware of the sensitivity of the issue and anxious to move on from the subject, went on, 'Now, we need to discuss these stories. I like them very much and believe they could do well. Have you thought about illustrations at all?'

'I hadn't got that far,' said Rod.

'I think they could work well as picture books,' went on Fanella, 'for the slightly older child who's beginning to read independently. But we'll need to adjust the length of some of them and one or two other details if they're to appeal to an international market.'

Rod could hardly believe his ears. International market! Illustrations! It all sounded so much grander than he'd imagined. He felt hugely grateful to Fanella for having so much faith in him, but there was still a worrying doubt at the back of his mind. If he was found guilty of hurting Dan, if the authority went against him, surely Fanella, or her publishers, wouldn't want to take him on as a children's author. He would be seen as a corrupting influence. It wouldn't do their sales any good at all to have their name connected to a child abuser.

At that moment, the waiter arrived with their food. They ate in silence for a few minutes. Fanella looked up at

Rod, wondering what was going on in his mind. He suddenly seemed very quiet, and she wondered if she'd said something to upset him. Perhaps he didn't like the idea of having to change his stories. Some authors never wanted to alter any of their precious work, even if their editors knew it would help to sell the books.

'Are you all right?' she said at last, unable to bear the silence any longer.

Rod glanced up at her. He sat back in his chair and took a deep breath. 'Look,' he said. 'All this is very exciting for me – the thought of having my stories published, of becoming a children's author. To tell you the truth, it's one of my lifetime ambitions. But I can't help feeling . . . perhaps this isn't a good time to be attempting it. You know, my name could be mud in a few weeks and you might regret taking me on.'

Fanella put her knife and fork down and looked at the handsome sensitive face across the table. Goodness, how he made her heart race! She would like to lean across and kiss him then and there. His deep dark eyes looked into hers, as if desperate for some reassurance, and seemed to hint at an equally deep soul. She couldn't have felt more certain that this man would be the last man on earth to hurt a little boy, however annoyed he might have been.

'I . . . As far as I'm concerned, there's no question about your innocence,' she burst out. 'I trust my feelings about people. It's how I knew Ellie would be the right child for me. It's how I knew you'd be the right teacher for her.'

'It's how I know you're the right man for me,' she continued silently. She looked into his eyes, hoping she hadn't revealed too much already.

73

'That's really sweet of you,' said Rod, looking back at Fanella's intense angry face across the table and feeling, as he had once before, that he'd like to know her better. She must be incredibly strong, he reflected, to have taken on a child on her own. Now she was revealing further strength: strength of belief in him as a teacher and a writer.

Fanella felt herself blush. Perhaps she had sounded too passionate; she didn't want him to know her true feelings. It would be terrible if he were to think she was only interested in meeting him because she had romantic fantasies about him. He was married, and although she could not hide her desire for him from herself, she must hide it from him. Otherwise he would suspect her of hidden motives, not only for this meeting, but also for believing him to be innocent.

Fanella pulled herself together. 'Publishing is a long drawn-out business,' she said, trying to make the meeting more businesslike. 'By the time we've got anywhere with your stories, this whole business at the school will have been long forgotten.'

'Right,' said Rod. 'Well, you know what you're doing and I trust you to use your own judgement.'

'Good,' said Fanella. 'Now, would you like a dessert?'

It was still raining when, an hour later, they left the restaurant.

'Do you need a lift somewhere?' asked Rod. 'My car's parked just around the corner.'

'It's OK,' said Fanella, rather regretting that she had her bike, 'I'm cycling.'

'Well, don't get too wet,' said Rod.

They stood hesitating for a few seconds, not sure how to end the meeting.

'Will you let me know the outcome of the hearing?' Fanella said, wanting to know for certain she would have contact with him again before too long. 'You've got my work number, haven't you?'

'Yes,' said Rod. 'Sure, I'll let you know. You've been very supportive.'

'And you'll send me the changes to your stories as soon as possible?'

'Oh yes,' said Rod. 'I'll get working on them straight away. Hey,' he added, as she turned to leave. He had grabbed hold of her arm and it sent an electric current flowing through her. 'Thank you,' he said, as she turned back to look at him.

Fanella smiled. 'It's nothing,' she said.

'No, really,' he said. 'It means a lot to me to know that some people still have confidence in me!'

Fanella smiled. Then, with a huge effort, she got onto her bike and rode away from him. It was as if a million invisible chains were pulling her towards him and she had to pedal extra hard to get back to work.

What an impossible situation! The more she saw of him, the stronger her feelings became. It would be better for her if she could forget all about him; better for Mark too, who she suddenly remembered had left a message for her to ring him that morning.

So why was she allowing herself to get more involved in Rod's life? It would all end in tears, she knew that. Yet she couldn't help herself: already she was plotting new opportunities to meet him, excuses to discuss his stories further with him. It was as if she were caught in a storm at sea and could do nothing to fight the currents that drew her towards him.

She got back to the office to find that Mark had rung her again. She had hardly given him any thought at all lately, poor man, although it seemed he was becoming keener on her by the day. She rang him back.

'I thought I'd come round this evening, and cook you and Ellie dinner,' he said.

He was clearly making an effort with Ellie now. He had realised, Fanella supposed, that if he wanted Fanella in his life he had to include Ellie in it too.

'That'd be lovely,' said Fanella.

She wanted to want him so much. He was, after all, available, good-looking and attracted to her. It was clear that he was a more suitable companion for her and Ellie than Rod was. Everything would be perfect if only she didn't feel so much for Rod! She decided she would try her best to turn her feelings in the direction of Mark. It must be possible to be rational about these things.

And, by the time she cycled home with Ellie later that afternoon, she felt quite certain that things with Mark were going to work. From now on, she would think of Rod simply as someone she did business with.

Chapter 12   *Betrayal!*

Rod drove home in a state of confusion. He drove slowly – it had started to rain heavily and he could hardly see the road ahead. He thought about Fanella and tried to sort out his feelings for her. On the one hand, he felt reassured by Fanella's obvious confidence in him; on the other, he was concerned that she didn't know what she was letting herself in for, by having so much faith in him.

There was something else that was worrying him, but he didn't know what it was exactly. Something about Fanella gave him feelings he would rather not have. He felt a warm affection for her, which made him want to protect her in some way. He knew this was irrational: after all, one of the things that had struck him about her at lunch today was her strength. He knew she was an independent woman who could stand on her own two feet perfectly well. She made him feel alive again and he was attracted to her, as if somehow he could be responsible for her happiness. But he didn't like to think about it: he had a wonderful wife at home.

As he drew nearer his home, he began to think of the good news he could relate to Leah about his stories. She would be proud of him, he was sure. Lately she seemed to have lost some of her respect for him, even though she knew he had not hurt Dan. It was as if, along with losing his job, however temporarily, he had lost some of his manliness. She didn't seem to want him near her very often, and she was spending more of her days out at clients' houses.

She would not have had the car today, however, and he was looking forward to arriving home as he used to, and finding her in her office, perhaps with a meal in the oven. Their roles would be more as they always had been, and he felt certain that the news about his stories would help them get back to normal.

As he turned into the driveway, he realised that a large car was parked in his usual space, and he would have to park out in the lane. He reversed and parked, and then, bending his head against the continuing heavy rain, ran towards the front door. Suddenly, something made him stop. The sound of the rain, obviously having drowned out the sound of his approaching footsteps, meant that Leah and her companion were completely unaware of his arrival.

Leah was in the arms of Mr Simpson from the farmhouse up the hill, her blonde head held back slightly, her eyes shut, as she kissed him on the lips. Rod had no time to think what to do. At that second, Leah opened her eyes, saw him and pulled quickly away from the man who, on seeing her look of alarm, swung round and came face to face with Rod.

For a few seconds the three of them stood in shocked silence. Then Mr Simpson climbed into his car as if nothing had happened, reversed down the drive, turned and drove fast up the hill towards his home.

Leah and Rod were left, the rain dripping off their hair, face to face with each other. Rod looked at Leah and felt himself strangely unmoved by what he had witnessed. It was as if the bits of a puzzle were suddenly falling into place, as if Leah was taking on a character he had always known was there, but had refused to acknowledge fully.

He walked past her into the house, surprised at himself for angrily pushing her aside as he went. He dropped his briefcase on the floor and went to the drinks cabinet. He poured himself a large whisky and sat on the sofa. Anger flowed through him, not anger at Leah, but at himself for having been so blind for so long.

Leah stood in the doorway. Her hair was untidy from the rain and from her passionate embrace with the farmer, and her feet were bare. She had clearly only slipped her boots on in order to say goodbye to him. In fact, now Rod thought about it, she had probably only just thrown her clothes on before he had arrived home.

'What can I say?' Leah began, apologetically. 'I didn't expect you home just then. I'm sorry you had to witness that. I really am.'

'You mean, you think it was better for me not to know?' asked Rod.

'Well . . . with your job and everything . . . I was going to tell you, but then I thought on top of all your other stresses at the moment, it was better for you not to know,' said Leah.

'How very thoughtful of you,' said Rod.

'Seriously Rod,' Leah went on, coming to sit beside him on the sofa and putting her arms round him for the first time in weeks, 'I wanted to tell you. It's been terrible keeping this secret from you for so long, but I just didn't think you'd be able to bear it on top of everything else.'

'So how long has this been going on?' asked Rod.

Strangely, he felt relieved to think it hadn't started as a result of what had happened to him at school.

'Ever since I first got the contract with him,' Leah said. 'I may as well tell you now: we'd been attracted to each other for a while before that, but neither of us had admitted how we felt.'

Rod sighed. It all made sense, he realised. There had been other clues which he had chosen to ignore: her annoyance at having him at home, the way she took so much trouble over her appearance when she was supposed to be at home all day.

It didn't stop his feelings of hurt and rejection, but he had to admit that they'd been drifting apart for some time. Even he had wondered at times if they would survive as a couple. They were so different! But he had always felt lucky that she was interested in him: she with her beauty and talent and wealth, attracted to a simple school teacher. It had been like a fairy story. He was so thankful for her interest, he had chosen to blind himself to the obvious barriers between them.

'So . . . what are we going to do?' he asked, looking at her, admiring her amazing looks and feeling that he could hardly blame other men for finding her attractive.

'I don't know, Rod,' she said, putting her head on his shoulder. 'I do love you, you know. I didn't want to spoil what we've got together. It's just that you've been so distant lately, and with your talk of wanting children and everything, I began to think we were from different worlds. There are certain areas in which I know I can never make you happy, such as giving you a child. You know I don't want children and I shan't change my mind.'

'That's OK,' said Rod. 'I realise that. Having a child isn't my only goal in life. I was willing to accept we wouldn't ever have any of our own.'

'But you'd be such a good father, it's a waste!' said Leah, and they both laughed a little.

'You mean you wanted me to go off and have children with someone else?' Rod asked.

'No!' said Leah sharply. 'But I have felt awful for denying you that opportunity.'

'So you decided to have an affair yourself?' said Rod. He tried not to sound bitter. 'What is it about him?' he asked, suddenly wondering.

'I don't know,' said Leah, withdrawing her arm from Rod's shoulders. 'I just like him. And his children are grown-up, so he's got all that stuff out of the way. It isn't an issue between us.'

'I see,' said Rod.

He suddenly felt exhausted. Whichever way he looked at it, it seemed like this was the end for him and Leah. And that was suddenly too much on top of everything else. No job, no marriage, no status. This was how people sank to the bottom of the heap.

He went and filled up his glass and drank it down in one go, then filled it again. 'I had some good news I was going to tell you,' he said, sitting back down beside her. 'I thought it might impress you, and that you would start to respect me again.' He realised he sounded self-pitying, like a little child, but he couldn't stop himself. 'But there's no point in telling you now.'

'Oh go on!' said Leah. 'We both need some good news. This hasn't been easy for me either, you know, with you at home and worrying about what's going to happen to you.'

'Well,' said Rod, 'the publisher is interested in my stories. Nothing's definite yet. But it's a good beginning. Now I've said it, it sounds completely meaningless.'

'Well done,' said Leah, but Rod could tell she didn't really consider this the best news she had ever heard.

'Are you going to leave me?' he asked, looking at her now and realising he sounded like the self-pitying little boy again.

'Rod, I think we may as well accept this is the end,' she said, and only then did he put his head down and begin to cry.

Chapter 13 *A dinner ruined*

Mark had brought salmon, salad, potatoes and ice cream with him to the house. He stood in Fanella's kitchen chopping and mixing, frying and roasting, while Fanella sat with Ellie playing 'Snap!' in the front room.

'Why does he have to be here?' Ellie asked crossly, as Fanella gave out the cards.

'He's cooking our supper,' said Fanella. 'It's good. It means I'm free to play cards with you.'

'We could have got a takeaway,' said Ellie who, Fanella was learning, had an answer to everything.

'Well, I think this will be nicer than a takeaway,' said Fanella. 'Mark's making salmon fishcakes.'

'Yuck!' said Ellie. 'I wanted a spring roll from the Chinese takeaway.'

'Oh come on, Ellie,' said Fanella, feeling that she might lose patience if she wasn't careful. 'It's kind of Mark to cook for us. And I want you to try and be polite to him. Even if you don't like the food.'

'Lie, you mean?'

'No, I don't mean you have to lie,' Fanella said.

'But if I'm polite, that means I will have to say I like the food when I don't, and that would be a lie!'

Fanella growled playfully. 'If you don't like the food, just say so politely,' she said. 'You could say, "Thank you very much Mark, but I don't like fishcakes".'

'OK,' said Ellie, suddenly becoming quite agreeable.

Fanella couldn't help feeling sorry for Mark as they sat down at his beautifully prepared table in the kitchen. He put a plate of fishcakes in front of them both, decorated with green herbs and a delicate Thai sauce he had made. Ellie waited for him to sit down before saying in her most grown-up voice, 'Thank you very much Mark, but I don't like fishcakes.'

Mark looked at the little girl and frowned. 'You could try them before you say you don't like them,' he said.

Fanella knew Mark had spoken to Ellie in the wrong way and that this would annoy her rather than calm her.

'If I know I don't like them, why should I try them?' she said.

'Because I said so,' said Mark. Clearly he was used to speaking to his own children this way.

'But you aren't my dad, you aren't even my teacher, so I don't have to do what you say,' said Ellie. And she kicked the table leg.

'Ellie!' said Fanella, feeling herself go hot. She knew she could have calmed Ellie down if Mark had not been there, but she was aware of his disapproving look. He obviously thought she was too soft on the child, and she found herself trying to please him. She spoke to Ellie in a way she thought he would approve of.

'Go to your room,' she said, and added, 'At once!' in the strictest voice she had ever used with her.

It was a mistake. Ellie pushed her chair back and threw her plate of food onto the floor, so that the plate smashed and the food flew all over the place. Then she burst into tears and ran upstairs. Fanella could hear her crying in her room as she swept up the broken plate.

'What that child needs is discipline,' said Mark. 'Don't be fooled by her crying, it's all an act. Ignore it. She'll soon be down for her supper.'

Fanella was not so sure. She had never sent Ellie to her room before, and if ever Ellie had been upset about something she had gone and comforted her. It felt wrong to ignore her, but she found it hard to argue with Mark.

They ate in silence. When they had finished, Mark came round to her side of the table and put his arms around her. 'Don't worry so much about the child,' he said, kissing her neck. 'She'll be fine. Now come on, let's go and make ourselves comfortable in the sitting room.'

It didn't feel right to Fanella, letting Mark kiss her while Ellie was upstairs on her own, but part of her felt she needed this. It was so hard bringing up a child on her own and although she didn't agree with Mark's approach, it felt reassuring to have him there, supporting her, letting her lean on him. Perhaps he was right that she should not let Ellie get away with so much. Perhaps ignoring her behaviour was the only way to deal with it.

She leant against Mark's broad shoulder and let him put his arms around her, and suddenly she realised how much she had missed adult contact over the months since Steven had left. She turned her face towards him and kissed him back, feeling the warmth of his lips against hers, and enjoying the strength of his arms around her.

It was a few minutes before she looked up and found herself face to face with Ellie. She was standing in the doorway, holding her teddy bear tightly, with her eyes swollen from crying.

Fanella leapt up. 'Come here, Ellie,' she said, opening

her arms wide and wanting nothing more than to hold the troubled child.

But Ellie froze in the doorway. Fanella went to her and knelt down, gently putting her arms around her. 'It's all right,' she said. 'Everything's all right.'

'I want him to go,' said Ellie, pointing at Mark.

'No, Ellie. Come on. Mark doesn't have to go. Why don't you make friends with him?'

Fanella rather hoped Mark would take this hint and say something playful to Ellie to indicate that he wanted to be friends with her. But he seemed incapable of getting onto her level.

'It's OK, Fanella,' he said. 'I'll go. I'll give you a ring and we'll meet again when Ellie is out at school.' He stared angrily at the little girl as he said this and she frowned back at him.

He picked up his coat and went out of the door, kissing Fanella on the cheek as he passed her. He squeezed her arm and she appreciated the reassurance he was clearly trying to communicate to her.

When he had gone, she took Ellie's hand and led her to the door. 'Let's go and get you that spring roll,' she said. She knew that she was going back on all that she had said to her earlier but decided that she should follow her own feelings. Ellie looked up at her and smiled.

Chapter 14 *The kiss*

On Monday morning Fanella was busy in the office when the telephone rang.

'Could I speak to Fanella Browning?'

Fanella felt a shiver run down her back. It was Rod, but she didn't want him to know that she recognised his voice. 'Speaking. Who is it?' she asked.

'Rod . . . I've made some corrections to my stories,' he said. 'Shall I send them to you?'

'Perhaps it's better if we meet again,' Fanella found herself saying, 'so that we can discuss the changes. When could you make it?'

'You say,' said Rod. 'I'm a man of leisure, remember?'

Fanella thought she noticed a bitterness in his voice she had never heard before, but chose to ignore it.

'Well, as soon as possible, I suppose,' she said. 'How about tomorrow? Could you come to my office?'

'OK. What time?'

'Say . . . eleven?'

'OK, I'll see you then.' And before she had time to say any more, he had put the phone down.

Fanella found that she was shaking. Something about Rod's manner had upset her. It was as if he was revealing a side of himself she hadn't seen before – a rather sharp angry side – and she wondered what had happened to him. He must be finding it very hard being at home all day.

Perhaps she was making a mistake accepting his stories at the moment. Perhaps she should wait until after his disciplinary hearing – it couldn't be that long now. She had no doubt about his innocence, but it might be better to let the air clear before she took him on as an author.

Still, she reminded herself, she was not agreeing to anything by meeting him tomorrow. She would remain cool and professional. For this reason, it was better to meet in the office than in a restaurant.

The next day, Rod arrived looking more untidy than usual. He hadn't shaved and his clothes looked as if he hadn't bothered to iron them. Fanella indicated a chair beside her and he threw the stories onto her desk rather carelessly.

'Are you OK?' she asked, looking at him questioningly.

He sat down and said, 'So–so. How about you? And Ellie? I do think about Ellie.'

'We're fine,' said Fanella. 'Waiting for the legalisation of the adoption which is a bit worrying, but otherwise we're OK. She'll be glad when you're back at school.'

'If,' said Rod, looking down at his hands.

They spent an hour going through his stories and Fanella approved the changes he'd made to them. He had listened well to her views, and the stories were greatly improved.

'So,' said Rod, 'what happens next?'

'I'll take them to an editorial meeting,' said Fanella. 'Then, if they are approved, they'll have to go to the sales people. That'll be the hard bit, because unless we get support there, I'm afraid we won't be able to publish them. It's a long time until then, though.'

She looked at him, waiting for him to stand up and say it was time for him to go. Their meeting had finished.

Rod glanced at her nervously. 'Do you fancy a quick walk along the river?' he asked. 'I could do with a bit of fresh air. Can you take some time off?'

Fanella hesitated. 'Well, it is my lunch hour now, so I guess I could go out for a bit. Yes, OK,' she said.

Despite his quiet mood, she still felt that invisible force which pulled her towards him. She was no more able to refuse an invitation for a walk with him than she would have been able to turn down the offer of a cold drink on a hot day.

She took her coat and followed him down the stairs and out into the windy May morning. They walked across Coe Fen, past the cows and on towards the river and the Anchor pub.

'I hope you don't mind,' Rod said, stopping suddenly and turning to face her. 'I wanted to talk to you. I can't keep everything inside any longer. It's so awful being at home every day and not seeing anyone.'

Fanella looked at him and wondered what on earth he was going to say. Was he about to confess that he had actually hit Dan, that he was not safe to work with children, that he had misled her?

She looked into his eyes and felt again the attraction she had felt so often before. She wondered if she would continue to feel like this, if she knew he had hit the little boy.

'I've been going through a bit of a rough time,' he said, beginning to walk again, looking at the footpath and kicking stones aside as he went. 'My marriage is in pieces, as well as my career, and I feel I'm losing my self-confidence. It's as if I'm on a slippery slope sliding faster and faster towards a muddy pool at the bottom.'

Fanella's stomach turned: since when had his marriage been in trouble? She knew this shouldn't make her feel happy, but suddenly it seemed like there might be some hope. 'But this is selfish of me,' she thought, looking at Rod's tired face. She tried to push away these feelings and instead give him the sympathy of a true friend.

'I know how you feel,' she said at last. 'I was going through a very similar crisis this time last year.'

'Really?' Rod was looking at her with desperation in his eyes, as if seeking a reassurance he could find nowhere else.

'Yes,' said Fanella.

'But look at you,' said Rod. 'You have a successful career; you're a strong independent woman; you're the last person I can imagine with low self-confidence.'

Fanella laughed, remembering the night Steven left her and the awful months when she felt a failure because she couldn't hold onto a relationship or have a child. She had believed she was the lowest of the low.

'This time last year,' she said, 'my boyfriend left me. We were trying to adopt a child together. He left me for a younger woman. I thought it was the end: the end of my relationship, the end of any hope of having a child, the end of any other potential relationships. But things have changed such a lot since then. You have to remember nothing lasts forever, not the good or the bad, and you have to hold onto yourself. You mustn't let other people's opinions affect you.'

'That's easy enough with people you don't respect,' said

Rod, 'but when your own wife seems to lose faith in you, you wonder whether she's right.'

'I haven't lost faith in you,' said Fanella at once, realising too late that it sounded as if she was competing with his wife for his affections.

He looked at her. 'That's why I feel I can talk to you,' he said. 'You always seem so calm, so sure about me. I really appreciate it.'

'Well,' said Fanella, suddenly not knowing where to look, 'it's because I . . . I . . . ' Suddenly she felt as if she had gone so far already, there was no point in holding back any more. 'I find you so . . . You were so sensitive with Ellie, and your stories are so good, and I know you'd never hurt any child, and I think you're beautiful, and clever and I . . . ' But before she could go any further, she felt his arms go around her and suddenly they were kissing.

She could feel the roughness of his chin against her cheek and the softness of his lips on hers. She smelt the warm male smell of his skin and she never wanted him to let her go.

After a few minutes he stood back and looked at her. 'Thank you,' he said. 'I've been wanting to do that for a long time.'

Then he took her in his arms once more and they kissed again. The sun came out and warmed their backs. For a short time, it was as if they were in another world where there was nothing but sunshine and blue sky and the warmth of one body against another.

But after a while, Rod stood back. 'I'd be in even more trouble if any of the parents at school saw me do this,' he said. 'We should be careful.'

'You're probably right,' said Fanella. 'But it's a shame. It's what I meant earlier when I said you mustn't let other people's opinions affect you.'

Rod looked at her and smiled. 'I've let your opinion affect me,' he said. 'It made me kiss you.'

'Well, good opinions are fine,' laughed Fanella, 'but not destructive ones. You have to reject them completely.'

She was burning from the feeling of his kiss and nothing could reduce the feeling of joy that had flooded through her the moment she felt his arms around her. She was lost in the moment and not thinking about realities – like the fact that she was seeing Mark, and the fact that Rod had only just been rejected by his wife and was no doubt looking for reassurance elsewhere.

When they parted, she to go back to the office, he to go home to his failed marriage, Fanella was still feeling as if she was walking on air. Reality would have to be faced but not now. It was not worth spoiling this wonderful moment so soon after experiencing it.

Chapter 15 *Fanella's choice*

On Saturday morning, Fanella and Teresa were walking along the River Cam towards Granchester. The two children ran ahead. Fanella had arranged to meet Mark at the Orchard Tea Rooms when they arrived. Teresa had suggested that they all go out together so that Mark could get to know the children better. Fanella was glad to have an opportunity to talk to Teresa.

Her meeting with Rod was two days ago and she hadn't heard from him since. But she hadn't stopped thinking about him. Her head was full of questions. What did the kiss mean? Did Rod have any feelings for her? Should she stop seeing Mark? She was bursting to tell Teresa what had happened. She thought if she could talk about it, she might be able to make things clearer in her head and decide what to do.

But it was Teresa who started the conversation. 'So how are things going with Mark?' she asked.

'Oh, not bad. He's good company,' said Fanella. 'I just wish he got on better with Ellie. But something else has happened and I think perhaps I should tell him. Teresa, it's about Rod. I've been longing to talk to someone about it.'

'Rod? He's not back at school is he?'

'No, not yet. But I've seen him a couple of times. He sent me some children's stories.'

'Oh?' Teresa sounded slightly surprised, and there was a hint of disapproval in her voice.

'So we had to meet and discuss them. They're very good, actually,' Fanella added.

Fanella suddenly found it difficult to get to the part of the story she most wanted to tell . . . about the kiss. She was aware that Teresa was a bit bad-tempered whenever she mentioned Rod, and suddenly wondered if she was the right person to tell. However, if she didn't tell Teresa there was certainly no-one else to talk to.

'Well, I didn't know he wrote stories himself,' said Teresa. 'I remember he asked you to go in and talk about publishing, so he had a hidden motive, did he?'

Teresa still sounded a little angry.

'No, I don't think he invited me just so he could get his stories published,' said Fanella. 'That just came up in a conversation we had afterwards. Anyway, we've met a couple of times since, and, oh, I don't know how to tell you this . . .'

'Go on,' said Teresa, suddenly suspicious.

'Well, last time we met we . . . kissed.' Fanella had said it! She felt a wave of relief.

But Teresa, when she spoke, sounded mistrusting. 'What do you mean, kissed?'

'Kissed. Oh come on, Teresa, you know what kissing is!'

'But it depends on the situation. I mean, did you just kiss each other goodbye on the cheek, or was it something more . . . passionate?'

'It was something more passionate.'

'Wow!' Teresa was silenced.

They walked along together for a few more minutes, then Teresa took a deep breath. 'You do know about his wife?' she said. 'I don't mean to sound disapproving, but I want to protect you, Fanella.'

'He's been having problems with his marriage: the relationship is falling apart,' said Fanella, trying to explain the whole situation in a few words.

'Since when?'

'Fairly recently. It seems to have been made worse by his suspension from school. His wife seems to have lost her respect for him'

'Oh, Fanella,' Teresa said. She stopped walking and turned to look at her friend seriously. 'You must realise what he's doing! Are you completely blind? A man who's just broken up with his beautiful wife, suffering from loss of confidence because his career may be over. He's just using you to build his self-confidence.'

'How can you possibly know that?' said Fanella, feeling suddenly angry. Why was Teresa so cross every time she mentioned Rod? She was supposed to be her best friend, and had always stood by her in the past. Teresa had helped her through all those times when she had discovered she couldn't have children, through trying to adopt with Steven and through their breakup. But now, suddenly, when she was about to find happiness, it was as if Teresa didn't like it one bit.

'It's just so obvious,' said Teresa, walking on again. 'And I would have thought it extremely unwise to get involved in publishing the children's stories of someone who's a possible child abuser.'

'Teresa!' Fanella looked at her friend disbelievingly. 'You don't mean to tell me you think he's guilty?'

'No, well, I mean we just don't know, do we? We shan't know until he's had his hearing. It's a nice thought that he's the innocent teacher, but we may be wrong.'

Fanella was speechless. She wished suddenly that she was somewhere else, not walking along to Granchester with Teresa. The floating feeling she'd had since Thursday had suddenly gone completely and the ground felt very hard beneath her feet.

At that moment, Ellie ran up to them. 'Can we feed the ducks? Have you got any bread?' she asked, and Fanella put her hand in her pocket for the old pieces of bread she had brought with her.

'Race you to the river!' said Ellie, and Fanella, using this as an excuse to get away from Teresa for a moment, chased Ellie towards the river, letting her win the race.

Later, in the tea room gardens, they sat under a tree on green deckchairs drinking coffee and eating chocolate cake. Mark arrived, and Ellie immediately looked at Timothy and made a face. Unfortunately, this was witnessed by all three adults.

Fanella felt embarrassed and tried to turn it into a joke. Teresa, who hadn't smiled since their earlier conversation, frowned even more deeply, and Mark, instead of ignoring it, chose to speak severely to the child. 'That is no way to welcome a friend of your mother's,' he said crossly to Ellie, who blushed deeply.

'Oh, come on, Mark,' began Fanella. 'She was only joking, weren't you darling?'

Ellie refused to speak.

'It's time she learnt that her mother's friends are to be

respected,' went on Mark. He looked huge standing over the children and staring angrily down at them.

Then he turned to Fanella. 'I'm surprised you're prepared to put up with her, Fanella.'

This was going too far. Ellie screwed up her face and shouted, 'She is not my mother! And you are not my mother's friend. I hate you!'

Mark went red with anger and raised his hand in the air above the child. Suddenly afraid, Ellie jumped out of her chair and ran towards the river.

Fanella didn't hesitate. She leapt up and, pushing Mark aside, ran after the little girl. She caught up with Ellie in a field full of cows and held her. The child was crying in despair.

'You are not my real mother and I hate that man,' she cried. 'I hate him. Why do you like him?'

Fanella held Ellie tightly. 'I don't like him any more,' she said. 'And I'm going to tell him so.'

Suddenly her love for Ellie was more important to her than anything else. Hearing Ellie say she wasn't her mother had hurt Fanella deeply because Ellie had been calling her 'Mummy' for some time now.

'Let's go home,' said Fanella, taking Ellie's hand. 'I'll talk to Mark and Teresa later.'

But Teresa was coming across the field towards them with Timothy following her. 'Oh dear!' Teresa said, coming up to Fanella. 'Mark's gone home. He said he'll call you later. Now come on, let's forget about it and go and finish our cake.' She stroked Ellie's hair, but Fanella suspected Teresa had partly agreed with Mark.

They ate their cake quietly, trying to regain some sense of peace. The Saturday morning sun warmed them as they ate and, after a while, Timothy and Ellie began to whisper and laugh together and the atmosphere softened. But there remained an awkward silence between Teresa and Fanella, and Fanella was quite relieved when Teresa decided it was time they went home.

*   *   *

It was early evening, and Ellie was happily lying on the floor watching *Snow White* on video when the doorbell rang. Fanella looked quickly out of the window to see that Mark was standing there, a bunch of flowers in his hands. Her heart sank.

Ellie was in the front room, so there was no way she could talk to Mark without Ellie hearing, or invite him into the kitchen without her seeing. She glanced at Ellie and, seeing that she was completely lost in the film, opened the door and stepped out onto the pavement.

Mark bent down and kissed her on the lips. She let him kiss her for a moment before moving back, and he handed her the flowers. 'These are to apologise for this morning,' he said. 'I realise I was wrong to criticise the way you deal with your child.'

Fanella looked at her feet. 'I can't take them,' she said. 'I'm sorry Mark, but I can't see you any more. Our relationship just isn't working.'

'I hope you're not letting that child's opinion affect you,' said Mark, holding her shoulder and looking deeply into her eyes. 'Fanella, you're a lovely woman and I'm falling in love with you. But you cannot sacrifice your happiness for the sake of a child.'

Fanella hated this kind of situation. She had rarely had to reject anyone. In fact, she hadn't done it since she was a teenager. She suddenly realised it was easier being walked out on than telling someone else to go.

'It's not just because of Ellie,' she said. 'I'm not ready for this kind of relationship. I need some space to be by myself.'

'But I've given you lots of space, haven't I?' continued Mark. 'I've hardly pressurised you. But I've been thinking about you more and more, and each time we say goodbye I can't wait to see you again. I haven't felt like this about anyone for years. It seems to me that Ellie is the only thing that stops us being very happy together, and if you could only show her how to behave . . . '

'Mark, I'm sorry. It's over.' Fanella found herself using the very words Steven had used to her.

Mark stared at her, letting her words sink in. Then he grabbed her and kissed her forcefully on the lips. Fanella gave in for a moment. But the memory of Rod's kiss was still clear in her mind and Mark's embrace meant nothing in comparison. She pulled away from him. But not before a BMW parked a little way down the street drove off into the summer evening.

Mark left then, and Fanella closed the door behind him and went to sit beside Ellie, who put her head on her shoulder. Together they watched as Snow White, having eaten the poisoned apple, was woken by the kiss of the handsome prince.

Chapter 16   *Another kiss*

The day Rod and Fanella had kissed, Rod had left feeling happy but confused. He had arrived home to find Leah waiting for him at the door. 'Hi!' she said, putting her arms up around his neck, and kissing him more affectionately than she had done for some time.

Rod was surprised and not completely displeased. He loved Leah, but at that moment he felt closer to Fanella.

'Rod,' said Leah, 'we need to talk. I've been thinking. I spoke too quickly the other day when I said it was over. I do still love you, and it isn't easy to throw a relationship away as quickly as this. Since I said we should finish, you've hardly been here, and I realise how much I miss you.'

Rod looked at her. She was so lovely, so beautiful, so intelligent. But he felt something was missing. Was it simply that he wasn't sure she meant what she said? Or had there always been something missing from their relationship? Something he hadn't noticed until he had kissed Fanella that afternoon.

'You certainly know how to surprise me,' said Rod, smiling.

'Let's talk later,' said Leah, beginning to kiss Rod again and leading him gently to the stairs. 'I feel like going to bed, don't you?'

'Hey, hang on,' said Rod. 'What's going on? Mr Simpson hasn't finished with you, has he?'

'No!' said Leah in a hurt voice. 'But I'm thinking of

finishing with him. It's you I really want. I've been doing a lot of thinking, and I realise that now.'

'Sorry,' said Rod. 'But I'm just not in the mood for bed. I've been feeling really bad about myself for a few weeks now, and I can't suddenly pretend everything's all right. I need to think, and we need to talk some more before we make any big decisions about our future.'

He released himself from her arms and poured himself a whisky. Then, taking his shoes off, he sat down on the sofa. 'I think we need to take a bit of a break, at least until my hearing next week,' he said. 'You may feel differently if I'm found guilty.'

'I shan't,' said Leah. 'I realise I haven't been very loyal to you throughout this, and I can see now that I should have stood by you. I do believe you're innocent, Rod, I really do.'

Rod looked at her and again felt confused about his feelings.

'How were your stories received today?' Leah then asked. It was the first time she had taken any interest in them.

'They were received very well,' said Rod. 'But there's still a long way to go, and I shan't feel confident until the hearing is over. The publishers won't want them if they find out I hit a child in my class.'

'But you didn't,' said Leah.

'Well, you and I know that,' said Rod.

'And I'm sure they'll find you innocent.'

'It's good of you to have confidence in me,' said Rod. He put his arm around her. 'I appreciate it.'

The whisky was warming his blood, and with Leah suddenly being so nice to him, he felt a huge weight lift off his shoulders.

Perhaps things were going to get better at last. He wondered if he should tell Leah what had happened that afternoon. But it was impossible to talk to her about it now. He hadn't had a chance to examine his own feelings yet, and if she knew about it, she might decide she was better-off without him after all. He put his head on Leah's shoulder. 'Give me a chance to think things through,' he said. 'We both need time after all that has happened.'

That weekend, Rod realised he still hadn't got Fanella out of his mind. He knew it was crazy. After all, his own wife wanted him back now and he loved her. But he couldn't leave a woman like Fanella waiting for some word from him. He was sure she must be wondering what on earth he was doing. He must see her somehow, and he must see her at once.

One problem was he didn't have Fanella's home address. He could wait until Monday and contact her at her office, but two days had already passed and he was aware that after their passionate embrace, his silence must look strange. Then he had an idea. He had taken the register at school every day and the children's addresses were written at the front. He hadn't seen the register for weeks, but he had a good memory. If he could just picture the front of the register, he would remember Ellie's address.

He concentrated hard, running down the list of names mentally: Kelly O'Neill, Timothy Paolotti, Grace Peters, until he got to Ellie's and then pictured the address next to it. Aha! He had it! He was certain of the street name but he couldn't remember the house number. But it wasn't a very long street and he was sure there would be some clue as to the right house if he went there.

He felt quite nervous as he turned into Fanella's street and began to drive slowly along, looking for a clue as to which house front was hers. He thought he might look rather suspicious to anyone watching him, and decided to park. He would wait and watch for a while. If nothing happened to indicate where she lived, he would get out and walk up and down the street until he spotted the house which must be hers. He wasn't sure what he was going to say to her if he found her, he just knew he had to see her. It was as if he was being pulled towards her by some invisible force.

A little while later, just as he was about to get out of the car and begin to walk, something caught his eye in his rear view mirror. Someone was standing outside the door of a house across the street holding a bunch of flowers in his hands. As he watched, Rod saw the door open and Fanella step out onto the pavement. The man holding the flowers kissed her, and she seemed to return the kiss. Rod's heart sank. He continued to watch. They seemed to be engaged in conversation for a while, before they put their arms round each other and kissed again, a long kiss this time. Rod didn't wait to see any more.

What a fool he had been! Of course Fanella must be seeing someone! She was too lovely and attractive to be left alone for long.

He drove away, feeling more upset than he had imagined possible. After all, when he had arrived in her street, he wasn't even sure what he wanted to see her for. But now, as he drove away, he realised he needed her. But it was no good. He wasn't about to interfere in her life, which was obviously complicated enough already, and make things even more confusing for her. He must stay away from her. She had enough to do with Ellie. She should be left to get on with forming a relationship with someone single and more suitable.

He drove out of town, away from the traffic, towards the open countryside, towards his home. He wished he felt happier that his beautiful wife seemed to want him back.

Chapter 17 *A wonderful surprise*

Teresa was on her way to school with Timothy.

'Have you heard?' another mother called out to her. 'Rod's back in school.'

'So he was found innocent?' Teresa asked. 'Of course, we all knew he would be.'

'Of course,' said the other mother. 'Apparently, the child who accused him admitted he'd lied. He did it to please his mother who seems to hate Rod for some reason.'

Teresa couldn't help feeling pleased that Rod was back in school. However, part of her was a little guilty that she hadn't defended him as loyally as Fanella had done.

As she arrived at the school gates, she saw that Fanella and Ellie were approaching on their bicycles. She hadn't seen Fanella since the awful day in Granchester, and she suddenly felt embarrassed. She wanted to leave Timothy and disappear quickly, but they all entered the classroom together.

'You're back!' Fanella said to Rod, blushing as she looked at him. Rod smiled at her. So, thought Teresa, Fanella didn't know Rod was back at school. It was obvious then, that they hadn't seen each other since their kiss. Teresa wasn't surprised.

'Yes, I'm back,' he said. 'Hello, Ellie. Hello, Timothy.' The two children smiled and ran to the book corner. For once Ellie was happy to be left.

'Well, we are truly pleased to see you,' said Teresa. 'I'll

catch up with you later, Fanella,' she said and left. Teresa felt she would rather not stand around witnessing the uncomfortable atmosphere between Rod and Fanella.

Fanella, who had not heard a thing from Rod since their meeting, was astonished to find him in school that morning. It was not exactly the right situation in which to bring up matters of the heart, but she found it hard to leave without referring at all to their recent meeting.

'I was wondering what had happened to you,' she said quietly, hoping the children couldn't hear. 'I was hoping you were OK.'

Rod looked at her. She was so kind and sensitive. He wished he could ask her to meet him again, but now he knew she was involved with someone else, it was impossible. And he still had to sort things out with Leah.

'I've just been very busy with one thing and another,' he said. 'I'm sorry.'

'That's OK,' said Fanella, her heart sinking. It was clear he wasn't about to ask her to meet him.

She must go before she made a fool of herself. Teresa had been right about his motives for kissing her that day. He must have needed some reassurance and used her to provide it. She left with a heavy heart.

Then suddenly, later that week, something happened which made her happier than she had ever been – and it had nothing to do with Rod. Her adoption of Ellie had been finalised and made legal. Ellie was as delighted as Fanella was.

'Can I have a party to celebrate being your proper daughter now?' Ellie asked Fanella.

'Of course you can, darling,' said Fanella. 'That's a great idea. We'll make some invitations and you can invite whoever you like from school.'

It was fun preparing for a party, and a huge relief to know that Ellie was hers properly, at last. Fanella longed to phone Teresa straight away and tell her the news, but things had been awkward between them recently. She felt a little lonely having so few people to share the good news with, but tried to concentrate on preparing a really good party for Ellie.

On the day of the party, Fanella and Ellie spent the whole morning getting dressed up. 'I'm going to do your hair, Mummy,' shouted Ellie. She had become increasingly excited as the day of the party drew near and was now almost uncontrollable. But Fanella didn't want to spoil her new daughter's fun.

'Go on then!' she said, and let Ellie tie little coloured ribbons all over her hair. Ellie then got some face paints and Fanella let her draw patterns all over her face. Fanella looked really odd by the time Ellie had finished but Ellie was happy, and that was all that mattered.

As the first guests arrived, they were amazed at the colourful sight at the door: Ellie in a pink ballet dress with her hair full of ribbons and Fanella's brightly coloured face, her hair also full of ribbons. The house was like a fairy castle inside, with balloons attached to every surface.

Ellie's friends arrived quickly one after the other. There were lots of little girls and a few boys, and some of their parents. Then Teresa arrived with Timothy and kissed Fanella warmly on the cheek. 'I'm so happy for you,' she said, and Fanella wished she'd phoned her before. 'Is Mark coming?' Teresa asked, following Fanella into the kitchen to get a drink.

Fanella laughed. 'I'd be really embarrassed if he saw me dressed like this!' she said. 'No, he isn't coming. It's all over.'

'So, you've definitely finished with him?' Teresa asked.

'Yes,' said Fanella, 'but you were right about Rod, too. It was just a one-off. He was obviously feeling low and in need of a little comfort. I'm sorry I didn't listen to you, I really am. I'm not seeing anyone, and it's probably a good thing. My priority now is to get Ellie really happy and settled and to strengthen our relationship.'

'I do think you're brave,' said Teresa, putting her arm around her friend. 'Not many people would cope as well as you on their own.'

Fanella grinned. 'The good thing about being single,' she said, 'is you can dress how you want and not care what anyone else thinks!'

'I must go to the toilet,' said Teresa, leaving Fanella alone in the kitchen wishing that what she had said about being single felt truer to her than it did.

Her thoughts were interrupted by Ellie's excited voice. 'Mummy, look who's here!'

Fanella looked up. There in the doorway, looking slightly self-conscious and holding a bottle of champagne, stood Rod! Ellie held his other hand.

'I didn't tell you I'd invited him, did I?' said Ellie, dancing around Rod. 'I thought it'd be a nice surprise!'

'It certainly is,' said Fanella, not bothering to hide her pleasure at seeing him. 'It's a wonderful surprise.'

'Because now you don't like Mark any more, I think Rod should be your friend,' said Ellie.

Rod and Fanella laughed, embarrassed, and Rod came across the kitchen and kissed Fanella on the cheek. 'Congratulations,' he said. 'Ellie is a very lucky girl finding a mummy like you, and you're lucky finding a girl like Ellie.' Ellie disappeared then, leaving her new mother and Rod looking at each other.

'So, "you don't like Mark any more",' he said, smiling and looking into her eyes.

Fanella smiled. 'He was just someone I saw for a while. Ellie couldn't stand him and you know children have a sense about these things. I realised she was right and broke it off the other day. It's a huge relief, actually.'

'So we've both broken off with people recently,' said Rod. 'My wife wanted us to get together again, but since I met you, I've been unable to think of anyone else. In a strange way I felt I'd be betraying her if I got back together with her. Fanella, I don't know how you feel, but I'm in love with you, and I need to see you. Is there any chance at all?'

Fanella was speechless. She looked at Rod disbelievingly. Then he began to laugh. 'It's the first time I've ever declared love for someone dressed like you are!' he said.

Fanella put her hands to her face in horror.

'No, don't wipe it off, I like it,' he said. 'It's a reminder of Ellie's creative talent.' And they began to kiss.

Chapter 18 *The sound of laughter*

'So,' said Ellie, running along beside Timothy in the park. 'I've got a mummy and a daddy now.'

'It seems strange your daddy being our teacher!' said Timothy.

'Mmm,' said Ellie, 'but I knew they were right for each other.'

Timothy laughed and ran off and Ellie followed.

Rod and Fanella walked a little way behind them, hand in hand.

'What's strange,' said Rod, looking down at Fanella, 'is that suddenly I've now got a child as well as you. I hadn't realised how much was missing from my life. Leah didn't want children, and while we were happy together I was willing to go along with her. But once things started to go wrong, I realised how important it was that I should be a father one day.'

'Do you mind that I can't have my own children?' Fanella asked him, searching his face for an honest reaction.

'Not at all. Ellie has come ready-made and I couldn't ask for a nicer daughter. And I knew the situation when I came into it.'

'But Rod, what would you say if I told you that actually the doctors must have made a mistake? That it must have been Steven who was partly responsible for my being unable to have children? What would you say, I mean, if I told you I was pregnant?'

Rod looked at her.

'You're not though, are you?' he said, barely able to hide the excitement in his voice.

'I am,' said Fanella, looking at him shyly.

Rod lifted Fanella up and swung her round. 'That's fantastic!' he said.

'I haven't told Ellie, and we'll have to be careful because she might get very jealous. But if we make it absolutely clear that she's our first child and extra special because I chose her, I think she'll cope.'

'Cope! I think she'll be the proudest child around. A new mother, a new father and a new brother or sister! It's the best thing I've heard in years!'

Just then Teresa arrived, waving at them as she came across the park. 'Thanks for having Timothy this morning,' she said, smiling at the couple. 'He thinks it a huge honour to be taken out by Fanella and his teacher.'

She smiled at Fanella. 'You two look the picture of happiness. Is there something I should know?'

Fanella and Rod looked at each other.

'I could give you a clue,' said Fanella. 'But no, I'll let you guess.'

Teresa gave Fanella a puzzled look. Once she knew Rod and Fanella had finally got together, all her doubts about them as a couple had disappeared. It suddenly seemed so obvious that they were made for each other, and although she still found him attractive herself, Teresa no longer felt the slightest bit jealous. It was so nice seeing Fanella happy and it was good to have Rod as a proper friend. So, now that they seemed to have even more good news, she felt genuinely excited for them.

'What on earth can it be?' she asked. Then her heart sank. 'You're not moving away somewhere?' she asked nervously.

She certainly did not want to lose them as friends.

'No,' said Fanella, 'although we may have to move into a bigger house. Two bedrooms won't be enough for us any more.'

'You're . . . adopting another child?' said Teresa.

'No.'

'You aren't . . . you aren't . . . Fanella, you're pregnant!'

Fanella nodded, smiling. 'Just shows you, doctors can be wrong.'

Teresa opened her arms wide and held her friend. 'That's fantastic!' she said, smiling at both of them. 'I'm so pleased for you. I wish I could stay to celebrate, but we're meeting Paulo and we're already late!' She called across to Timothy and then turned back to the happy couple. 'Congratulations, the pair of you!' she said as Timothy and Ellie ran up together, laughing and out of breath.

Teresa and Timothy said goodbye and walked towards the road. On reaching their parked car, they turned to wave one final goodbye. The little trio waved back: Rod on one side, Fanella on the other and Ellie in the middle. The two adults took hold of Ellie's hands and swung her high into the air. All Teresa could hear, as she opened the car door for Timothy, was the sound of their laughter as they moved together across the park.